*THE THREE TAVERNS*
*DIONYSUS IN DOUBT*

THE MACMILLAN COMPANY
NEW YORK · BOSTON · CHICAGO · DALLAS
ATLANTA · SAN FRANCISCO

MACMILLAN & CO., LIMITED
LONDON · BOMBAY · CALCUTTA
MELBOURNE

THE MACMILLAN CO. OF CANADA, LTD.
TORONTO

# COLLECTED POEMS

*THE THREE TAVERNS*
*DIONYSUS IN DOUBT*

By EDWIN ARLINGTON ROBINSON

THE MACMILLAN COMPANY

NEW YORK        MCMXXVII

# CONTENTS

[ v ]

# THE THREE TAVERNS
## (1920)

*To*
*Thomas  Sergeant  Perry*
*and  Lilla  Cabot  Perry*

# THE VALLEY OF THE SHADOW

There were faces to remember in the Valley of the Shadow,
There were faces unregarded, there were faces to forget;
There were fires of grief and fear that are a few forgotten, ashes,
There were sparks of recognition that are not forgotten yet.
For at first, with an amazed and overwhelming indignation
At a measureless malfeasance that obscurely willed it thus,
They were lost and unacquainted—till they found themselves
    in others,
Who had groped as they were groping where dim ways were
    perilous.

There were lives that were as dark as are the fears and intuitions
Of a child who knows himself and is alone with what he knows;
There were pensioners of dreams and there were debtors of
    illusions,
All to fail before the triumph of a weed that only grows.
There were thirsting heirs of golden sieves that held not wine
    or water,
And had no names in traffic or more value there than toys:

There were blighted sons of wonder in the Valley of the Shadow,
Where they suffered and still wondered why their wonder made
no noise.

There were slaves who dragged the shackles of a precedent
unbroken,
Demonstrating the fulfilment of unalterable schemes,
Which had been, before the cradle, Time's inexorable ten-
ants
Of what were now the dusty ruins of their father's dreams.
There were these, and there were many who had stumbled up
to manhood,
Where they saw too late the road they should have taken
long ago:
There were thwarted clerks and fiddlers in the Valley of the
Shadow,
The commemorative wreckage of what others did not know.

And there were daughters older than the mothers who had borne
them,
Being older in their wisdom, which is older than the earth;
And they were going forward only farther into darkness,
Unrelieved as were the blasting obligations of their birth;

And among them, giving always what was not for their pos-
    session,
There were maidens, very quiet, with no quiet in their eyes;
There were daughters of the silence in the Valley of the Shadow,
Each an isolated item in the family sacrifice.

There were creepers among catacombs where dull regrets were
    torches,
Giving light enough to show them what was there upon the
    shelves—
Where there was more for them to see than pleasure would
    remember
Of something that had been alive and once had been them-
    selves.
There were some who stirred the ruins with a solid imprecation,
While as many fled repentance for the promise of despair:
There were drinkers of wrong waters in the Valley of the
    Shadow,
And all the sparkling ways were dust that once had led them
    there.

There were some who knew the steps of Age incredibly beside
    them,

And his fingers upon shoulders that had never felt the wheel;
And their last of empty trophies was a gilded cup of nothing,
Which a contemplating vagabond would not have come to steal.
Long and often had they figured for a larger valuation,
But the size of their addition was the balance of a doubt:
There were gentlemen of leisure in the Valley of the Shadow,
Not allured by retrospection, disenchanted, and played out.

And among the dark endurances of unavowed reprisals
There were silent eyes of envy that saw little but saw well;
And over beauty's aftermath of hazardous ambitions
There were tears for what had vanished as they vanished where
    they fell.
Not assured of what was theirs, and always hungry for the
    nameless,
There were some whose only passion was for Time who made
    them cold:
There were numerous fair women in the Valley of the Shadow,
Dreaming rather less of heaven than of hell when they were old.

Now and then, as if to scorn the common touch of common
    sorrow,
There were some who gave a few the distant pity of a smile;

And another cloaked a soul as with an ash of human embers,
Having covered thus a treasure that would last him for a while.
There were many by the presence of the many disaffected,
Whose exemption was included in the weight that others bore:
There were seekers after darkness in the Valley of the Shadow,
And they alone were there to find what they were looking for.

So they were, and so they are; and as they came are coming
    others,
And among them are the fearless and the meek and the unborn;
And a question that has held us heretofore without an answer
May abide without an answer until all have ceased to mourn.
For the children of the dark are more to name than are the
    wretched,
Or the broken, or the weary, or the baffled, or the shamed:
There are builders of new mansions in the Valley of the Shadow,
And among them are the dying and the blinded and the mained.

# THE WANDERING JEW

I saw by looking in his eyes
That they remembered everything,
And this was how I came to know
That he was here, still wandering.
For though the figure and the scene
Were never to be reconciled,
I knew the man as I had known
His image when I was a child.

With evidence at every turn,
I should have held it safe to guess
That all the newness of New York
Had nothing new in loneliness;
Yet here was one who might be Noah,
Or Nathan, or Abimelech,
Or Lamech, out of ages lost,—
Or, more than all, Melchizedek.

Assured that he was none of these,
I gave them back their names again,
To scan once more those endless eyes
Where all my questions ended then.

I found in them what they revealed
That I shall not live to forget,
And they wondered if found in mine
Compassion that I might regret.


Pity, I learned, was not the least
Of time's offending benefits
That had now for so long impugned
The conservation of his wits:
Rather it was that I should yield,
Alone, the fealty that presents
The tribute of a tempered ear
To an untempered eloquence.


Before I pondered long enough
On whence he came and who he was,
I trembled at his ringing wealth
Of manifold anathemas;
I wondered, while he seared the world,
What new defection ailed the race,
And if it mattered how remote
Our fathers were from such a place.

[7]

Before there was an hour for me
To contemplate with less concern
The crumbling realm awaiting us
Than his that was beyond return,
A dawning on the dust of years
Had shaped with an elusive light
Mirages of remembered scenes
That were no longer for the sight.

For now the gloom that hid the man
Became a daylight on his wrath,
And one wherein my fancy viewed
New lions ramping in his path.
The old were dead and had no fangs,
Wherefore he loved them—seeing not
They were the same that in their time
Had eaten everything they caught.

The world around him was a gift
Of anguish to his eyes and ears,
And one that he had long reviled
As fit for devils, not for seers.
Where, then, was there a place for him
That on this other side of death

Saw nothing good, as he had seen
No good come out of Nazareth?

Yet here there was a reticence,
And I believe his only one,
That hushed him as if he beheld
A Presence that would not be gone.
In such a silence he confessed
How much there was to be denied;
And he would look at me and live,
As others might have looked and died.

As if at last he knew again
That he had always known, his eyes
Were like to those of one who gazed
On those of One who never dies.
For such a moment he revealed
What life has in it to be lost;
And I could ask if what I saw,
Before me there, was man or ghost.

He may have died so many times
That all there was of him to see

[ 9 ]

Was pride, that kept itself alive
As too rebellious to be free;
He may have told, when more than once
Humility seemed imminent,
How many a lonely time in vain
The Second Coming came and went.

Whether he still defies or not
The failure of an angry task
That relegates him out of time
To chaos, I can only ask.
But as I knew him, so he was;
And somewhere among men to-day
Those old, unyielding eyes may flash,
And flinch—and look the other way.

# NEIGHBORS

As often as we thought of her,
　　We thought of a gray life
That made a quaint economist
　　Of a wolf-haunted wife;
We made the best of all she bore
　　That was not ours to bear,
And honored her for wearing things
　　That were not things to wear.

There was a distance in her look
　　That made us look again;
And if she smiled, we might believe
　　That we had looked in vain.
Rarely she came inside our doors,
　　And had not long to stay;
And when she left, it seemed somehow
　　That she was far away.

At last, when we had all forgot
　　That all is here to change,
A shadow on the commonplace
　　Was for a moment strange.

Yet there was nothing for surprise,
  Nor much that need be told:
Love, with its gift of pain, had given
  More than one heart could hold.

# THE MILL

The miller's wife had waited long,
    The tea was cold, the fire was dead;
And there might yet be nothing wrong
    In how he went and what he said:
"There are no millers any more,"
    Was all that she had heard him say;
And he had lingered at the door
    So long that it seemed yesterday.

Sick with a fear that had no form
    She knew that she was there at last;
And in the mill there was a warm
    And mealy fragrance of the past.
What else there was would only seem
    To say again what he had meant;
And what was hanging from a beam
    Would not have heeded where she went.

And if she thought it followed her,
    She may have reasoned in the dark
That one way of the few there were
    Would hide her and would leave no mark:

[ 13 ]

Black water, smooth above the weir
Like starry velvet in the night,
Though ruffled once, would soon appear
The same as ever to the sight.

# THE DARK HILLS

Dark hills at evening in the west,
Where sunset hovers like a sound
Of golden horns that sang to rest
Old bones of warriors under ground,
Far now from all the bannered ways
Where flash the legions of the sun,
You fade—as if the last of days
Were fading, and all wars were done.

# THE THREE TAVERNS

When the brethren heard of us, they came to meet us as far as Appii
Forum, and The Three Taverns.

*(Acts xxviii, 15)*

Herodion, Apelles, Amplias,
And Andronicus?  Is it you I see—
At last?  And is it you now that are gazing
As if in doubt of me?  Was I not saying
That I should come to Rome?  I did say that;
And I said furthermore that I should go
On westward, where the gateway of the world
Lets in the central sea.  I did say that,
But I say only, now, that I am Paul—
A prisoner of the Law, and of the Lord
A voice made free.  If there be time enough
To live, I may have more to tell you then
Of western matters.  I go now to Rome,
Where Cæsar waits for me, and I shall wait,
And Cæsar knows how long.  In Cæsarea
There was a legend of Agrippa saying
In a light way to Festus, having heard
My deposition, that I might be free,
Had I stayed free of Cæsar; but the word

[ 16 ]

Of God would have it as you see it is—
And here I am.  The cup that I shall drink
Is mine to drink—the moment or the place
Not mine to say.  If it be now in Rome,
Be it now in Rome; and if your faith exceed
The shadow cast of hope, say not of me
Too surely or too soon that years and shipwreck,
And all the many deserts I have crossed
That are not named or regioned, have undone
Beyond the brevities of our mortal healing
The part of me that is the least of me.
You see an older man than he who fell
Prone to the earth when he was nigh Damascus,
Where the great light came down; yet I am he
That fell, and he that saw, and he that heard.
And I am here, at last; and if at last
I give myself to make another crumb
For this pernicious feast of time and men—
Well, I have seen too much of time and men
To fear the ravening or the wrath of either.

Yes, it is Paul you see—the Saul of Tarsus
That was a fiery Jew, and had men slain

For saying Something was beyond the Law,
And in ourselves.  I fed my suffering soul
Upon the Law till I went famishing,
Not knowing that I starved.  How should I know,
More then than any, that the food I had—
What else it may have been—was not for me?
My fathers and their fathers and their fathers
Had found it good, and said there was no other,
And I was of the line.  When Stephen fell,
Among the stones that crushed his life away,
There was no place alive that I could see
For such a man.  Why should a man be given
To live beyond the Law?  So I said then,
As men say now to me.  How then do I
Persist in living?  Is that what you ask?
If so, let my appearance be for you
No living answer; for Time writes of death
On men before they die, and what you see
Is not the man.  The man that you see not—
The man within the man—is most alive;
Though hatred would have ended, long ago,
The bane of his activities.  I have lived,
Because the faith within me that is life

Endures to live, and shall, till soon or late,
Death, like a friend unseen, shall say to me
My toil is over and my work begun.


How often, and how many a time again,
Have I said I should be with you in Rome!
He who is always coming never comes,
Or comes too late, you may have told yourselves;
And I may tell you now that after me,
Whether I stay for little or for long,
The wolves are coming.  Have an eye for them,
And a more careful ear for their confusion
Than you need have much longer for the sound
Of what I tell you—should I live to say
More than I say to Cæsar.  What I know
Is down for you to read in what is written;
And if I cloud a little with my own
Mortality the gleam that is immortal,
I do it only because I am I—
Being on earth and of it, in so far
As time flays yet the remnant.  This you know;
And if I sting men, as I do sometimes,
With a sharp word that hurts, it is because

Man's habit is to feel before he sees;
And I am of a race that feels.  Moreover,
The world is here for what is not yet here
For more than are a few; and even in Rome,
Where men are so enamored of the Cross
That fame has echoed, and increasingly,
The music of your love and of your faith
To foreign ears that are as far away
As Antioch and Haran, yet I wonder
How much of love you know, and if your faith
Be the shut fruit of words.  If so, remember
Words are but shells unfilled.  Jews have at least
A Law to make them sorry they were born
If they go long without it; and these Gentiles,
For the first time in shrieking history,
Have love and law together, if so they will,
For their defense and their immunity
In these last days.  Rome, if I know the name,
Will have anon a crown of thorns and fire
Made ready for the wreathing of new masters,
Of whom we are appointed, you and I,—
And you are still to be when I am gone,
Should I go presently.  Let the word fall,

Meanwhile, upon the dragon-ridden field
Of circumstance, either to live or die;
Concerning which there is a parable,
Made easy for the comfort and attention
Of those who preach, fearing they preach in vain.

You are to plant, and then to plant again
Where you have gathered, gathering as you go;
For you are in the fields that are eternal,
And you have not the burden of the Lord
Upon your mortal shoulders.  What you have
Is a light yoke, made lighter by the wearing,
Till it shall have the wonder and the weight
Of a clear jewel, shining with a light
Wherein the sun and all the fiery stars
May soon be fading.  When Gamaliel said
That if they be of men these things are nothing,
But if they be of God, they are for none
To overthrow, he spoke as a good Jew,
And one who stayed a Jew; and he said all.
And you know, by the temper of your faith,
How far the fire is in you that I felt
Before I knew Damascus.  A word here,

Or there, or not there, or not anywhere,
Is not the Word that lives and is the life;
And you, therefore, need weary not yourselves
With jealous aches of others. If the world
Were not a world of aches and innovations,
Attainment would have no more joy of it.
There will be creeds and schisms, creeds in creeds,
And schisms in schisms; myriads will be done
To death because a farthing has two sides,
And is at last a farthing. Telling you this,
I, who bid men to live, appeal to Cæsar.
Once I had said the ways of God were dark,
Meaning by that the dark ways of the Law.
Such is the Glory of our tribulations;
For the Law kills the flesh that kills the Law,
And we are then alive. We have eyes then;
And we have then the Cross between two worlds—
To guide us, or to blind us for a time,
Till we have eyes indeed. The fire that smites
A few on highways, changing all at once,
Is not for all. The power that holds the world
Away from God that holds himself away—
Farther away than all your works and words

Are like to fly without the wings of faith—
Was not, nor ever shall be, a small hazard
Enlivening the ways of easy leisure
Or the cold road of knowledge.   When our eyes
Have wisdom, we see more than we remember;
And the old world of our captivities
May then become a smitten glimpse of ruin,
Like one where vanished hewers have had their day
Of wrath on Lebanon.   Before we see,
Meanwhile, we suffer; and I come to you,
At last, through many storms and through much night.

Yet whatsoever I have undergone,
My keepers in this instance are not hard.
But for the chance of an ingratitude,
I might indeed be curious of their mercy,
And fearful of their leisure while I wait,
A few leagues out of Rome.   Men go to Rome,
Not always to return—but not that now.
Meanwhile, I seem to think you look at me
With eyes that are at last more credulous
Of my identity.   You remark in me
No sort of leaping giant, though some words

Of mine to you from Corinth may have leapt
A little through your eyes into your soul.
I trust they were alive, and are alive
To-day; for there be none that shall indite
So much of nothing as the man of words
Who writes in the Lord's name for his name's sake
And has not in his blood the fire of time
To warm eternity.  Let such a man—
If once the light is in him and endures—
Content himself to be the general man,
Set free to sift the decencies and thereby
To learn, except he be one set aside
For sorrow, more of pleasure than of pain;
Though if his light be not the light indeed,
But a brief shine that never really was,
And fails, leaving him worse than where he was,
Then shall he be of all men destitute.
And here were not an issue for much ink,
Or much offending faction among scribes.

The Kingdom is within us, we are told;
And when I say to you that we possess it
In such a measure as faith makes it ours,

I say it with a sinner's privilege
Of having seen and heard, and seen again,
After a darkness; and if I affirm
To the last hour that faith affords alone
The Kingdom entrance and an entertainment,
I do not see myself as one who says
To man that he shall sit with folded hands
Against the Coming.  If I be anything,
I move a driven agent among my kind,
Establishing by the faith of Abraham,
And by the grace of their necessities,
The clamoring word that is the word of life
Nearer then heretofore to the solution
Of their tomb-serving doubts.  If I have loosed
A shaft of language that has flown sometimes
A little higher than the hearts and heads
Of nature's minions, it will yet be heard,
Like a new song that waits for distant ears.
I cannot be the man that I am not;
And while I own that earth is my affliction,
I am a man of earth, who says not all
To all alike.  That were impossible,
Even as it were so that He should plant

A larger garden first.  But you to-day
Are for the larger sowing; and your seed,
A little mixed, will have, as He foresaw,
The foreign harvest of a wider growth,
And one without an end.  Many there are,
And are to be, that shall partake of it,
Though none may share it with an understanding
That is not his alone.  We are all alone;
And yet we are all parcelled of one order—
Jew, Gentile, or barbarian in the dark
Of wildernesses that are not so much
As names yet in a book.  And there are many,
Finding at last that words are not the Word,
And finding only that, will flourish aloft,
Like heads of captured Pharisees on pikes,
Our contradictions and discrepancies;
And there are many more will hang themselves
Upon the letter, seeing not in the Word
The friend of all who fail, and in their faith
A sword of excellence to cut them down.

As long as there are glasses that are dark—
And there are many—we see darkly through them;

All which have I conceded and set down
In words that have no shadow.  What is dark
Is dark, and we may not say otherwise;
Yet what may be as dark as a lost fire
For one of us, may still be for another
A coming gleam across the gulf of ages,
And a way home from shipwreck to the shore;
And so, through pangs and ills and desperations,
There may be light for all.  There shall be light.
As much as that, you know.  You cannot say
This woman or that man will be the next
On whom it falls; you are not here for that.
Your ministration is to be for others
The firing of a rush that may for them
Be soon the fire itself.  The few at first
Are fighting for the multitude at last;
Therefore remember what Gamaliel said
Before you, when the sick were lying down
In streets all night for Peter's passing shadow.
Fight, and say what you feel; say more than words.
Give men to know that even their days of earth
To come are more than ages that are gone.
Say what you feel, while you have time to say it.

Eternity will answer for itself,
Without your intercession; yet the way
For many is a long one, and as dark,
Meanwhile, as dreams of hell.  See not your toil
Too much, and if I be away from you,
Think of me as a brother to yourselves,
Of many blemishes.  Beware of stoics,
And give your left hand to grammarians;
And when you seem, as many a time you may,
To have no other friend than hope, remember
That you are not the first, or yet the last.

The best of life, until we see beyond
The shadows of ourselves (and they are less
Than even the blindest of indignant eyes
Would have them) is in what do we not know.
Make, then, for all your fears a place to sleep
With all your faded sins; nor think yourselves
Egregious and alone for your defects
Of youth and yesterday.  I was young once;
And there's a question if you played the fool
With a more fervid and inherent zeal
Than I have in my story to remember,

Or gave your necks to folly's conquering foot,
Or flung yourselves with an unstudied aim,
More frequently than I.  Never mind that.
Man's little house of days will hold enough,
Sometimes, to make him wish it were not his,
But it will not hold all.  Things that are dead
Are best without it, and they own their death
By virtue of their dying.  Let them go,—
But think you not the world is ashes yet,
And you have all the fire.  The world is here
To-day, and it may not be gone to-morrow;
For there are millions, and there may be more,
To make in turn a various estimation
Of its old ills and ashes, and the traps
Of its apparent wrath.  Many with ears
That hear not yet, shall have ears given to them,
And then they shall hear strangely.  Many with eyes
That are incredulous of the Mystery
Shall yet be driven to feel, and then to read
Where language has an end and is a veil,
Not woven of our words.  Many that hate
Their kind are soon to know that without love
Their faith is but the perjured name of nothing.

I that have done some hating in my time
See now no time for hate; I that have left,
Fading behind me like familiar lights
That are to shine no more for my returning,
Home, friends, and honors,—I that have lost all else
For wisdom, and the wealth of it, say now
To you that out of wisdom has come love,
That measures and is of itself the measure
Of works and hope and faith. Your longest hours
Are not so long that you may torture them
And harass not yourselves; and the last days
Are on the way that you prepare for them,
And was prepared for you, here in a world
Where you have sinned and suffered, striven and seen.
If you be not so hot for counting them
Before they come that you consume yourselves,
Peace may attend you all in these last days—
And me, as well as you. Yes, even in Rome.

Well, I have talked and rested, though I fear
My rest has not been yours; in which event,
Forgive one who is only seven leagues
From Cæsar. When I told you I should come,

I did not see myself the criminal
You contemplate, for seeing beyond the Law
That which the Law saw not.  But this, indeed,
Was good of you, and I shall not forget;
No, I shall not forget you came so far
To meet a man so dangerous.  Well, farewell.
They come to tell me I am going now—
With them.  I hope that we shall meet again,
But none may say what he shall find in Rome.

# DEMOS

## I

All you that are enamored of my name
    And least intent on what most I require,
    Beware; for my design and your desire,
Deplorably, are not as yet the same.
Beware, I say, the failure and the shame
    Of losing that for which you now aspire
    So blindly, and of hazarding entire
The gift that I was bringing when I came.

Give as I will, I cannot give you sight
    Whereby to see that with you there are some
    To lead you, and be led.  But they are dumb
Before the wrangling and the shrill delight
    Of your deliverance that has not come,
And shall not, if I fail you—as I might.

# DEMOS

## II

So little have you seen of what awaits
    Your fevered glimpse of a democracy
    Confused and foiled with an equality
Not equal to the envy it creates,
That you see not how near you are the gates
    Of an old king who listens fearfully
    To you that are outside and are to be
The noisy lords of imminent estates.

Rather be then your prayer that you shall have
    Your kingdom undishonored.  Having all,
    See not the great among you for the small,
But hear their silence; for the few shall save
    The many, or the many are to fall—
Still to be wrangling in a noisy grave.

# THE FLYING DUTCHMAN

Unyielding in the pride of his defiance,
    Afloat with none to serve or to command,
Lord of himself at last, and all by Science,
    He seeks the Vanished Land.

Alone, by the one light of his one thought,
    He steers to find the shore from which we came,
Fearless of in what coil he may be caught
    On seas that have no name.

Into the night he sails; and after night
    There is a dawning, though there be no sun;
Wherefore, with nothing but himself in sight,
    Unsighted, he sails on.

At last there is a lifting of the cloud
    Between the flood before him and the sky;
And then—though he may curse the Power aloud
    That has no power to die—

He steers himself away from what is haunted
    By the old ghost of what has been before,—
Abandoning, as always, and undaunted,
    One fog-walled island more.

[ 34 ]

# TACT

Observant of the way she told
    So much of what was true,
No vanity could long withhold
    Regard that was her due:
She spared him the familiar guile,
    So easily achieved,
That only made a man to smile
    And left him undeceived.

Aware that all imagining
    Of more than what she meant
Would urge an end of everything,
    He stayed; and when he went,
They parted with a merry word
    That was to him as light
As any that was ever heard
    Upon a starry night.

She smiled a little, knowing well
    That he would not remark
The ruins of a day that fell
    Around her in the dark:

[ 35 ]

He saw no ruins anywhere,
    Nor fancied there were scars
On anyone who lingered there,
    Alone below the stars.

# ON THE WAY

(PHILADELPHIA, 1794)

Note.—The following imaginary dialogue between Alexander Hamilton and Aaron Burr, which is not based upon any specific incident in American history, may be supposed to have occurred a few months previous to Hamilton's retirement from Washington's Cabinet in 1795 and a few years before the political ingenuities of Burr—who has been characterized, without much exaggeration, as the inventor of American politics—began to be conspicuously formidable to the Federalists. These activities on the part of Burr resulted, as the reader will remember, in the Burr-Jefferson tie for the Presidency in 1800, and finally in the Burr-Hamilton duel at Weehawken in 1804.

## BURR

Hamilton, if he rides you down, remember
That I was here to speak, and so to save
Your fabric from catastrophe. That's good;
For I perceive that you observe him also.
A President, a-riding of his horse,
May dust a General and be forgiven;
But why be dusted—when we're all alike,
All equal, and all happy? Here he comes—
And there he goes. And we, by your new patent,
Would seem to be two kings here by the wayside,
With our two hats off to his Excellency.
Why not his Majesty, and done with it?

Forgive me if I shook your meditation,
But you that weld our credit should have eyes
To see what's coming.   Bury me first if *I* do.

### HAMILTON

There's always in some pocket of your brain
A care for me; wherefore my gratitude
For your attention is commensurate
With your concern.   Yes, Burr, we are two kings;
We are as royal as two ditch-diggers;
But owe me not your sceptre.   These are the days
When first a few seem all; but if we live
We may again be seen to be the few
That we have always been.   These are the days
When men forget the stars, and are forgotten.

### BURR

But why forget them?   They're the same that winked
Upon the world when Alcibiades
Cut off his dog's tail to induce distinction.
There are dogs yet, and Alcibiades
Is not forgotten.

## HAMILTON

Yes, there are dogs enough,
God knows; and I can hear them in my dreams.

## BURR

Never a doubt.  But what you hear the most
Is your new music, something out of tune
With your intention.  How in the name of Cain,
I seem to hear you ask, are men to dance,
When all men are musicians.  Tell me that,
I hear you saying, and I'll tell you the name
Of Samson's mother.  But why shroud yourself
Before the coffin comes?  For all you know,
The tree that is to fall for your last house
Is now a sapling.  You may have to wait
So long as to be sorry; though I doubt it,
For you are not at home in your new Eden
Where chilly whispers of a likely frost
Accumulate already in the air.
I think a touch of ermine, Hamilton,
Would be for you in your autumnal mood
A pleasant sort of warmth along the shoulders.

[ 39 ]

## HAMILTON

If so it is you think, you may as well
Give over thinking.   We are done with ermine.
What I fear most is not the multitude,
But those who are to loop it with a string
That has one end in France and one end here.
I'm not so fortified with observation
That I could swear that more than half a score
Among us who see lightning see that ruin
Is not the work of thunder.   Since the world
Was ordered, there was never a long pause
For caution between doing and undoing.

## BURR

Go on, sir; my attention is a trap
Set for the catching of all compliments
To Monticello, and all else abroad
That has a name or an identity.

## HAMILTON

I leave to you the names—there are too many;
Yet one there is to sift and hold apart,
As now I see.   There comes at last a glimmer

That is not always clouded, or too late.
But I was near and young, and had the reins
To play with while he manned a team so raw
That only God knows where the end had been
Of all that riding without Washington.
There was a nation in the man who passed us,
If there was not a world. I may have driven
Since then some restive horses, and alone,
And through a splashing of abundant mud;
But he who made the dust that sets you on
To coughing, made the road. Now it seems dry,
And in a measure safe.

BURR

    Here's a new tune
From Hamilton. Has your caution all at once,
And over night, grown till it wrecks the cradle?
I have forgotten what my father said
When I was born, but there's a rustling of it
Among my memories, and it makes a noise
About as loud as all that I have held
And fondled heretofore of your same caution.
But that's affairs, not feelings. If our friends

[ 41 ]

Guessed half we say of them, our enemies
Would itch in our friends' jackets.  Howsoever,
The world is of a sudden on its head,
And all are spilled—unless you cling alone
With Washington.  Ask Adams about that.

### HAMILTON

We'll not ask Adams about anything.
We fish for lizards when we choose to ask
For what we know already is not coming.
And we must eat the answer.  Where's the use
Of asking when this man says everything,
With all his tongues of silence?

### BURR

                              I dare say.
I dare say, but I won't.  One of those tongues
I'll borrow for the nonce.  He'll never miss it.
We mean his Western Majesty, King George.

### HAMILTON

I mean the man who rode by on his horse.
I'll beg of you the meed of your indulgence
If I should say this planet may have done

A deal of weary whirling when at last,
If ever, Time shall aggregate again
A majesty like his that has no name.

### BURR

Then you concede his Majesty?  That's good,
And what of yours?   Here are two majesties.
Favor the Left a little, Hamilton,
Or you'll be floundering in the ditch that waits
For riders who forget where they are riding.
If we and France, as you anticipate,
Must eat each other, what Cæsar, if not yourself,
Do you see for the master of the feast?
There may be a place waiting on your head
For laurel thick as Nero's.   You don't know.
I have not crossed your glory, though I might
If I saw thrones at auction.

### HAMILTON

                    Yes, you might.
If war is on the way, I shall be—here;
And I've no vision of your distant heels.

## BURR

I see that I shall take an inference
To bed with me to-night to keep me warm.
I thank you, Hamilton, and I approve
Your fealty to the aggregated greatness
Of him you lean on while he leans on you.

## HAMILTON

This easy phrasing is a game of yours
That you may win to lose.  I beg your pardon,
But you that have the sight will not employ
The will to see with it.  If you did so,
There might be fewer ditches dug for others
In your perspective; and there might be fewer
Contemporary motes of prejudice
Between you and the man who made the dust.
Call him a genius or a gentleman.
A prophet or a builder, or what not,
But hold your disposition off the balance,
And weigh him in the light.  Once (I believe
I tell you nothing new to your surmise,
Or to the tongues of towns and villages)
I nourished with an adolescent fancy—

Surely forgivable to you, my friend—
An innocent and amiable conviction
That I was, by the grace of honest fortune,
A savior at his elbow through the war,
Where I might have observed, more than I did,
Patience and wholesome passion. I was there,
And for such honor I gave nothing worse
Than some advice at which he may have smiled.
I must have given a modicum besides,
Or the rough interval between those days
And these would never have made for me my friends,
Or enemies. I should be something somewhere—
I say not what—but I should not be here
If he had not been there. Possibly, too,
You might not—or that Quaker with his cane.

BURR

Possibly, too, I should. When the Almighty
Rides a white horse, I fancy we shall know it.

HAMILTON

It was a man, Burr, that was in my mind;
No god, or ghost, or demon—only a man:

[ 45 ]

A man whose occupation is the need
Of those who would not feel it if it bit them;
And one who shapes an age while he endures
The pin pricks of inferiorities;
A cautious man, because he is but one;
A lonely man, because he is a thousand.
No marvel you are slow to find in him
The genius that is one spark or is nothing:
His genius is a flame that he must hold
So far above the common heads of men
That they may view him only through the mist
Of their defect, and wonder what he is.
It seems to me the mystery that is in him
That makes him only more to me a man
Than any other I have ever known.

## BURR

I grant you that his worship is a man.
I'm not so much at home with mysteries,
May be, as you—so leave him with his fire:
God knows that I shall never put it out.
He has not made a cripple of himself
In his pursuit of me, though I have heard

His condescension honors me with parts.
Parts make a whole, if we've enough of them;
And once I figured a sufficiency
To be at least an atom in the annals
Of your republic.   But I must have erred.

## HAMILTON

You smile as if your spirit lived at ease
With error.   I should not have named it so,
Failing assent from you; nor, if I did,
Should I be so complacent in my skill
To comb the tangled language of the people
As to be sure of anything in these days.
Put that much in account with modesty.

## BURR

What in the name of Ahab, Hamilton,
Have you, in the last region of your dreaming,
To do with "people" ?   You may be the devil
In your dead-reckoning of what reefs and shoals
Are waiting on the progress of our ship
Unless you steer it, but you'll find it irksome
Alone there in the stern; and some warm day

There'll be an inland music in the rigging,
And afterwards on deck. I'm not affined
Or favored overmuch at Monticello,
But there's a mighty swarming of new bees
About the premises, and all have wings.
If you hear something buzzing before long,
Be thoughtful how you strike, remembering also
There was a fellow Naboth had a vineyard,
And Ahab cut his hair off and went softly.

HAMILTON

I don't remember that he cut his hair off.

BURR

Somehow I rather fancy that he did.
If so, it's in the Book; and if not so,
He did the rest, and did it handsomely.

HAMILTON

Commend yourself to Ahab and his ways
If they inveigle you to emulation;
But where, if I may ask it, are you tending
With your invidious wielding of the Scriptures?

[ 48 ]

You call to mind an eminent archangel
Who fell to make him famous.  Would you fall
So far as he, to be so far remembered?

## BURR

Before I fall or rise, or am an angel,
I shall acquaint myself a little further
With our new lands' new language, which is not—
Peace to your dreams—an idiom to your liking.
I'm wondering if a man may always know
How old a man may be at thirty-seven;
I wonder likewise if a prettier time
Could be decreed for a good man to vanish
Than about now for you, before you fade,
And even your friends are seeing that you have had
Your cup too full for longer mortal triumph.
Well, you have had enough, and had it young;
And the old wine is nearer to the lees
Than you are to the work that you are doing.

## HAMILTON

When does this philological excursion
Into new lands and languages begin?

[ 49 ]

### BURR

Anon—that is, already.  Only Fortune
Gave me this afternoon the benefaction
Of your blue back, which I for love pursued,
And in pursuing may have saved your life—
Also the world a pounding piece of news:
Hamilton bites the dust of Washington,
Or rather of his horse.  For you alone,
Or for your fame, I'd wish it might have been so.

### HAMILTON

Not every man among us has a friend
So jealous for the other's fame.  How long
Are you to diagnose the doubtful case
Of Demos—and what for?  Have you a sword
For some new Damocles?  If it's for me,
I have lost all official appetite,
And shall have faded, after January,
Into the law.  I'm going to New York.

### BURR

No matter where you are, one of these days
I shall come back to you and tell you something.

[ 50 ]

This Demos, I have heard, has in his wrist
A pulse that no two doctors have as yet
Counted and found the same, and in his mouth
A tongue that has the like alacrity
For saying or not for saying what most it is
That pullulates in his ignoble mind.
One of these days I shall appear again,
To tell you more of him and his opinions;
I shall not be so long out of your sight,
Or take myself so far, that I may not,
Like Alcibiades, come back again.
He went away to Phrygia, and fared ill.

HAMILTON

There's an example in Themistocles:
He went away to Persia, and fared well.

BURR

So?  Must I go so far?  And if so, why so?
I had not planned it so.  Is this the road
I take?  If so, farewell.

HAMILTON

      Quite so.  Farewell.

# JOHN BROWN

Though for your sake I would not have you now
So near to me to-night as now you are,
God knows how much a stranger to my heart
Was any cold word that I may have written;
And you, poor woman that I made my wife,
You have had more of loneliness, I fear,
Than I—though I have been the most alone,
Even when the most attended.  So it was
God set the mark of his inscrutable
Necessity on one that was to grope,
And serve, and suffer, and withal be glad
For what was his, and is, and is to be,
When his old bones, that are a burden now,
Are saying what the man who carried them
Had not the power to say.  Bones in a grave,
Cover them as they will with choking earth,
May shout the truth to men who put them there,
More than all orators.  And so, my dear,
Since you have cheated wisdom for the sake
Of sorrow, let your sorrow be for you,
This last of nights before the last of days,
The lying ghost of what there is of me

That is the most alive.   There is no death
For me in what they do.   Their death it is
They should heed most when the sun comes again
To make them solemn.   There are some I know
Whose eyes will hardly see their occupation,
For tears in them—and all for one old man;
For some of them will pity this old man,
Who took upon himself the work of God
Because he pitied millions.   That will be
For them, I fancy, their compassionate
Best way of saying what is best in them
To say; for they can say no more than that,
And they can do no more than what the dawn
Of one more day shall give them light enough
To do.   But there are many days to be,
And there are many men to give their blood,
As I gave mine for them.   May they come soon!

May they come soon, I say.   And when they come,
May all that I have said unheard be heard,
Proving at last, or maybe not—no matter—
What sort of madness was the part of me
That made me strike, whether I found the mark

Or missed it.  Meanwhile, I've a strange content,
A patience, and a vast indifference
To what men say of me and what men fear
To say.  There was a work to be begun,
And when the Voice, that I have heard so long,
Announced as in a thousand silences
An end of preparation, I began
The coming work of death which is to be,
That life may be.  There is no other way
Than the old way of war for a new land
That will not know itself and is to-night
A stranger to itself, and to the world
A more prodigious upstart among states
Than I was among men, and so shall be
Till they are told and told, and told again;
For men are children, waiting to be told,
And most of them are children all their lives.
The good God in his wisdom had them so,
That now and then a madman or a seer
May shake them out of their complacency
And shame them into deeds.  The major file
See only what their fathers may have seen,
Or may have said they saw when they saw nothing.

[ 54 ]

I do not say it matters what they saw.
Now and again to some lone soul or other
God speaks, and there is hanging to be done,—
As once there was a burning of our bodies
Alive, albeit our souls were sorry fuel.
But now the fires are few, and we are poised
Accordingly, for the state's benefit,
A few still minutes between heaven and earth.
The purpose is, when they have seen enough
Of what it is that they are not to see,
To pluck me as an unripe fruit of treason,
And then to fling me back to the same earth
Of which they are, as I suppose, the flower—
Not given to know the riper fruit that waits
For a more comprehensive harvesting.

Yes, may they come, and soon.   Again I say,
May they come soon!—before too many of them
Shall be the bloody cost of our defection.
When hell waits on the dawn of a new state,
Better it were that hell should not wait long,—
Or so it is I see it who should see
As far or farther into time to-night

Than they who talk and tremble for me now,
Or wish me to those everlasting fires
That are for me no fear.   Too many fires
Have sought me out and seared me to the bone—
Thereby, for all I know, to temper me
For what was mine to do.   If I did ill
What I did well, let men say I was mad;
Or let my name for ever be a question
That will not sleep in history.   What men say
I was will cool no cannon, dull no sword,
Invalidate no truth.   Meanwhile, I was;
And the long train is lighted that shall burn,
Though floods of wrath may drench it, and hot feet
May stamp it for a slight time into smoke
That shall blaze up again with growing speed,
Until at last a fiery crash will come
To cleanse and shake a wounded hemisphere,
And heal it of a long malignity
That angry time discredits and disowns.


To-night there are men saying many things;
And some who see life in the last of me

Will answer first the coming call to death;
For death is what is coming, and then life.
I do not say again for the dull sake
Of speech what you have heard me say before,
But rather for the sake of all I am,
And all God made of me.   A man to die
As I do must have done some other work
Than man's alone.   I was not after glory,
But there was glory with me, like a friend,
Throughout those crippling years when friends were few,
And fearful to be known by their own names
When mine was vilified for their approval.
Yet friends they are, and they did what was given
Their will to do; they could have done no more.
I was the one man mad enough, it seems,
To do my work; and now my work is over.
And you, my dear, are not to mourn for me,
Or for your sons, more than a soul should mourn
In Paradise, done with evil and with earth.
There is not much of earth in what remains
For you; and what there may be left of it
For your endurance you shall have at last
In peace, without the twinge of any fear

For my condition; for I shall be done
With plans and actions that have heretofore
Made your days long and your nights ominous
With darkness and the many distances
That were between us.  When the silence comes,
I shall in faith be nearer to you then
Than I am now in fact.  What you see now
Is only the outside of an old man,
Older than years have made him.  Let him die,
And let him be a thing for little grief.
There was a time for service and he served;
And there is no more time for anything
But a short gratefulness to those who gave
Their scared allegiance to an enterprise
That has the name of treason—which will serve
As well as any other for the present.
There are some deeds of men that have no names,
And mine may like as not be one of them.
I am not looking far for names to-night.
The King of Glory was without a name
Until men gave Him one; yet there He was,
Before we found Him and affronted Him
With numerous ingenuities of evil,

[ 58 ]

Of which one, with His aid, is to be swept
And washed out of the world with fire and blood.


Once I believed it might have come to pass
With a small cost of blood; but I was dreaming—
Dreaming that I believed.  The Voice I heard
When I left you behind me in the north,—
To wait there and to wonder and grow old
Of loneliness,—told only what was best,
And with a saving vagueness, I should know
Till I knew more.  And had I known even then—
After grim years of search and suffering,
So many of them to end as they began—
After my sickening doubts and estimations
Of plans abandoned and of new plans vain—
After a weary delving everywhere
For men with every virtue but the Vision—
Could I have known, I say, before I left you
That summer morning, all there was to know—
Even unto the last consuming word
That would have blasted every mortal answer
As lightning would annihilate a leaf,

I might have trembled on that summer morning;
I might have wavered; and I might have failed.

And there are many among men to-day
To say of me that I had best have wavered.
So has it been, so shall it always be,
For those of us who give ourselves to die
Before we are so parcelled and approved
As to be slaughtered by authority.
We do not make so much of what they say
As they of what our folly says of us;
They give us hardly time enough for that,
And thereby we gain much by losing little.
Few are alive to-day with less to lose
Than I who tell you this, or more to gain;
And whether I speak as one to be destroyed
For no good end outside his own destruction,
Time shall have more to say than men shall hear
Between now and the coming of that harvest
Which is to come.  Before it comes, I go—
By the short road that mystery makes long
For man's endurance of accomplishment.
I shall have more to say when I am dead.

[ 60 ]

# THE FALSE GODS

"We are false and evanescent, and aware of our deceit,
From the straw that is our vitals to the clay that is our feet.
You may serve us if you must, and you shall have your wage
    of ashes,—
Though arrears due thereafter may be hard for you to meet.

"You may swear that we are solid, and may say that we are
    strong,
But we know that we are neither and we say that you are
    wrong;
You may find an easy worship in acclaiming our indulgence,
But your large admiration of us now is not for long.

"If your doom is to adore us with a doubt that's never still,
And you pray to see our faces—pray in earnest, and you will.
You may gaze at us and live, and live assured of our confusion:
For the False Gods are mortal, and are made for you to kill.

"And you may as well observe, while apprehensively at ease
With an Art that's inorganic and is anything you please,
That anon your newest ruin may lie crumbling unregarded,
Like an old shrine forgotten in a forest of new trees.

"Howsoever like no other be the mode you may employ,

There's an order in the ages for the ages to enjoy;

Though the temples you are shaping and the passions you are
    singing

Are a long way from Athens and a longer way from Troy.


"When we promise more than ever of what never shall arrive,

And you seem a little more than ordinarily alive,

Make a note that you are sure you understand our obligations—

For there's grief always auditing where two and two are five.


"There was this for us to say and there was this for you to
    know,

Though it humbles and it hurts us when we have to tell you so.

If you doubt the only truth in all our perjured composition,

May the True Gods attend you and forget us when we go."

# ARCHIBALD'S EXAMPLE

Old Archibald, in his eternal chair,
Where trespassers, whatever their degree,
Were soon frowned out again, was looking off
Across the clover when he said to me:

"My green hill yonder, where the sun goes down
Without a scratch, was once inhabited
By trees that injured him—an evil trash
That made a cage, and held him while he bled.

"Gone fifty years, I see them as they were
Before they fell.  They were a crooked lot
To spoil my sunset, and I saw no time
In fifty years for crooked things to rot.

"Trees, yes; but not a service or a joy
To God or man, for they were thieves of light.
So down they came.  Nature and I looked on,
And we were glad when they were out of sight.

"Trees are like men, sometimes; and that being so,
So much for that."  He twinkled in his chair,
And looked across the clover to the place
That he remembered when the trees were there.

"Do I hear them?  Yes, I hear the children singing—and what
of it?
Have you come with eyes afire to find me now and ask me that?
If I were not their father and if you were not their mother,
We might believe they made a noise. . . . What are you—
driving at!"

"Well, be glad that you can hear them, and be glad they are so
near us,—
For I have heard the stars of heaven, and they were nearer still.
All within an hour it is that I have heard them calling,
And though I pray for them to cease, I know they never will;
For their music on my heart, though you may freeze it, will fall
always,
Like summer snow that never melts upon a mountain-top.
Do you hear them?  Do you hear them overhead—the children
—singing?
Do you hear the children singing? . . . God, will you make
them stop!"

"And what now in His holy name have you to do with moun-
tains?
We're back to town again, my dear, and we've a dance to-night.

Frozen hearts and falling music?  Snow and stars, and—what
    the devil!
Say it over to me slowly, and be sure you have it right."


"God knows if I be right or wrong in saying what I tell you,
Or if I know the meaning any more of what I say.
All I know is, it will kill me if I try to keep it hidden—
Well, I met him. . . . Yes, I met him, and I talked with him—
    to-day."


"You met him?  Did you meet the ghost of someone you had
    poisoned,
Long ago, before I knew you for the woman that you are?
Take a chair; and don't begin your stories always in the middle.
Was he man, or was he demon?  Anyhow, you've gone too far
To go back, and I'm your servant.  I'm the lord, but you're
    the master.
Now go on with what you know, for I'm excited."


                            "Do you mean—
Do you mean to make me try to think that you know less than
    I do?"

"I know that you foreshadow the beginning of a scene.

Pray be careful, and as accurate as if the doors of heaven

Were to swing or to stay bolted from now on for evermore."


"Do you conceive, with all your smooth contempt of every
feeling,

Of hiding what you know and what you must have known
before?

Is it worth a woman's torture to stand here and have you
smiling,

With only your poor fetish of possession on your side?

No thing but one is wholly sure, and that's not one to scare
me;

When I meet it I may say to God at last that I have tried.

And yet, for all I know, or all I dare believe, my trials

Henceforward will be more for you to bear than are your
own;

And you must give me keys of yours to rooms I have not entered.

Do you see me on your threshold all my life, and there alone?

Will you tell me where you see me in your fancy—when it
leads you

Far enough beyond the moment for a glance at the abyss?"

"Will you tell me what intrinsic and amazing sort of nonsense
You are crowding on the patience of the man who gives you—
    this?
Look around you and be sorry you're not living in an attic,
With a civet and a fish-net, and with you to pay the rent.
I say words that you can spell without the use of all your letters;
And I grant, if you insist, that I've a guess at what you meant."


"Have I told you, then, for nothing, that I met him? Are you
    trying
To be merry while you try to make me hate you?"

                                    "Think again,
My dear, before you tell me, in a language unbecoming
In a lady, what you plan to tell me next. If I complain,
If I seem an atom peevish at the preference you mention—
Or imply, to be precise—you may believe, or you may not,
That I'm a trifle more aware of what he wants than you are.
But I shouldn't throw that at you. Make believe that I
    forgot.
Make believe that he's a genius, if you like,—but in the mean-
    time
Don't go back to rocking-horses. There, there, there, now."

"Make believe!
When you see me standing helpless on a plank above a whirl-
    pool,
Do I drown, or do I hear you when you say it? Make believe?
How much more am I to say or do for you before I tell you
That I met him! What's to follow now may be for you to
    choose.
Do you hear me? Won't you listen? It's an easy thing to
    listen. . . ."


And it's easy to be crazy when there's everything to lose."


"If at last you have a notion that I mean what I am saying,
Do I seem to tell you nothing when I tell you I shall try?
If you save me, and I lose him—I don't know—it won't much
    matter.
I dare say that I've lied enough, but now I do not lie."


"Do you fancy me the one man who has waited and said
    nothing
While a wife has dragged an old infatuation from a tomb?
Give the thing a little air and it will vanish into ashes.
There you are—piff! presto!"

[ 68 ]

"When I came into this room,
It seemed as if I saw the place, and you there at your table,
As you are now at this moment, for the last time in my life;
And I told myself before I came to find you, 'I shall tell him,
If I can, what I have learned of him since I became his wife.'
And if you say, as I've no doubt you will before I finish,
That you have tried unceasingly, with all your might and
    main
To teach me, knowing more than I of what it was I needed,
Don't think, with all you may have thought, that you have tried
    in vain;
For you have taught me more than hides in all the shelves of
    knowledge
Of how little you found that's in me and was in me all along.
I believed, if I intruded nothing on you that I cared for,
I'd be half as much as horses,—and it seems that I was wrong;
I believed there was enough of earth in me, with all my non-
    sense
Over things that made you sleepy, to keep something still
    awake;
But you taught me soon to read my book, and God knows I
    have read it—
Ages longer than an angel would have read it for your sake.

I have said that you must open other doors than I have entered,
But I wondered while I said it if I might not be obscure.
Is there anything in all your pedigrees and inventories
With a value more elusive than a dollar's?  Are you sure
That if I starve another year for you I shall be stronger
To endure another like it—and another—till I'm dead?"


"Has your tame cat sold a picture?—or more likely had a
    windfall?
Or for God's sake, what's broke loose?  Have you a bee-hive
    in your head?
A little more of this from you will not be easy hearing
Do you know that?  Understand it, if you do; for if you
    won't. . . .
What the devil are you saying!  Make believe you never said it,
And I'll say I never heard it. . . . Oh, you. . . . If you. . . ."


                                        "If I don't?"


"There are men who say there's reason hidden somewhere in a
    woman,
But I doubt if God himself remembers where the key was
    hung."

[ 70 ]

"He may not; for they say that even God himself is growing.
I wonder if He makes believe that He is growing young;
I wonder if He makes believe that women who are giving
All they have in holy loathing to a stranger all their lives
Are the wise ones who build houses in the Bible. . . ."

                        "Stop—you devil!"

". . . Or that souls are any whiter when their bodies are called
    wives.
If a dollar's worth of gold will hoop the walls of hell together,
Why need heaven be such a ruin of a place that never
    was?
And if at last I lied my starving soul away to nothing,
Are you sure you might not miss it?  Have you come to such
    a pass
That you would have me longer in your arms if you dis-
    covered
That I made you into someone else. . . . Oh! . . . Well, there
    are worse ways.
But why aim it at my feet—unless you fear you may be
    sorry. . . .
There are many days ahead of you."

                    "I do not see those days."

"I can see them. Granted even I am wrong, there are the
    children.
And are they to praise their father for his insight if we die?
Do you hear them? Do you hear them overhead—the children
    —singing?
Do you hear them? Do you hear the children?"

                    "Damn the children!"

                                        "Why?
What have *they* done? . . . Well, then,—do it. . . . Do it now,
    and have it over."

"Oh, you devil! . . . Oh, you— . . ."

                        "No, I'm not a devil, I'm a prophet—
One who sees the end already of so much that one end more
Would have now the small importance of one other small
    illusion,
Which in turn would have a welcome where the rest have gone
    before.
But if I were you, my fancy would look on a little farther
For the glimpse of a release that may be somewhere still in sight.
Furthermore, you must remember those two hundred invitations
For the dancing after dinner. We shall have to shine to-night.

We shall dance, and be as happy as a pair of merry spectres,

On the grave of all the lies that we shall never have to tell;

We shall dance among the ruins of the tomb of our endurance,

And I have not a doubt that we shall do it very well.

There!—I'm glad you've put it back; for I don't like it.    Shut
the drawer now.

No—no—don't cancel anything.    I'll dance until I drop.

I can't walk yet, but I'm going to. . . . Go away somewhere,
and leave me. . . .

Oh, you children!  Oh, you children! . . . God, will they never
stop!"

# TASKER NORCROSS

"Whether all towns and all who live in them—
So long as they be somewhere in this world
That we in our complacency call ours—
Are more or less the same, I leave to you.
I should say less.  Whether or not, meanwhile,
We've all two legs—and as for that, we haven't—
There were three kinds of men where I was born:
The good, the not so good, and Tasker Norcross.
Now there are two kinds."

      "Meaning, as I divine,
Your friend is dead," I ventured.

        Ferguson,
Who talked himself at last out of the world
He censured, and is therefore silent now,
Agreed indifferently: "My friends are dead—
Or most of them."

      "Remember one that isn't,"
I said, protesting.  "Honor him for his ears;
Treasure him also for his understanding."

[ 74 ]

Ferguson sighed, and then talked on again:
"You have an overgrown alacrity
For saying nothing much and hearing less;
And I've a thankless wonder, at the start,
How much it is to you that I shall tell
What I have now to say of Tasker Norcross,
And how much to the air that is around you.
But given a patience that is not averse
To the slow tragedies of haunted men—
Horrors, in fact, if you've a skilful eye
To know them at their firesides, or out walking,—"

"Horrors," I said, "are my necessity;
And I would have them, for their best effect,
Always out walking."

                    Ferguson frowned at me:
"The wisest of us are not those who laugh
Before they know.  Most of us never know—
Or the long toil of our mortality
Would not be done.  Most of us never know—
And there you have a reason to believe
In God, if you may have no other.  Norcross,

Or so I gather of his infirmity,
Was given to know more than he should have known,
And only God knows why.  See for yourself
An old house full of ghosts of ancestors,
Who did their best, or worst, and having done it,
Died honorably; and each with a distinction
That hardly would have been for him that had it,
Had honor failed him wholly as a friend.
Honor that is a friend begets a friend.
Whether or not we love him, still we have him;
And we must live somehow by what we have,
Or then we die.  If you say chemistry,
Then you must have your molecules in motion,
And in their right abundance.  Failing either,
You have not long to dance.  Failing a friend,
A genius, or a madness, or a faith
Larger than desperation, you are here
For as much longer than you like as may be.
Imagining now, by way of an example,
Myself a more or less remembered phantom—
Again, I should say less—how many times
A day should I come back to you?  No answer.
Forgive me when I seem a little careless,

But we must have examples, or be lucid
Without them; and I question your adherence
To such an undramatic narrative
As this of mine, without the personal hook."

"A time is given in Ecclesiastes
For divers works," I told him. "Is there one
For saying nothing in return for nothing?
If not, there should be." I could feel his eyes,
And they were like two cold inquiring points
Of a sharp metal. When I looked again,
To see them shine, the cold that I had felt
Was gone to make way for a smouldering
Of lonely fire that I, as I knew then,
Could never quench with kindness or with lies.
I should have done whatever there was to do
For Ferguson, yet I could not have mourned
In honesty for once around the clock
The loss of him, for my sake or for his,
Try as I might; nor would his ghost approve,
Had I the power and the unthinking will
To make him tread again without an aim
The road that was behind him—and without

The faith, or friend, or genius, or the madness
That he contended was imperative.

After a silence that had been too long,
"It may be quite as well we don't," he said;
"As well, I mean, that we don't always say it.
You know best what I mean, and I suppose
You might have said it better.  What was that?
Incorrigible?  Am I incorrigible?
Well, it's a word; and a word has its use,
Or, like a man, it will soon have a grave.
It's a good word enough.  Incorrigible,
May be, for all I know, the word for Norcross.
See for yourself that house of his again
That he called home: an old house, painted white,
Square as a box, and chillier than a tomb
To look at or to live in.  There were trees—
Too many of them, if such a thing may be—
Before it and around it.  Down in front
There was a road, a railroad, and a river;
Then there were hills behind it, and more trees.
The thing would fairly stare at you through trees,
Like a pale inmate out of a barred window

With a green shade half down; and I dare say

People who passed have said: ' There's where he lives.

We know him, but we do not seem to know

That we remember any good of him,

Or any evil that is interesting.

There you have all we know and all we care.'

They might have said it in all sorts of ways;

And then, if they perceived a cat, they might

Or might not have remembered what they said.

The cat might have a personality—

And maybe the same one the Lord left out

Of Tasker Norcross, who, for lack of it,

Saw the same sun go down year after year;

All which at last was my discovery.

And only mine, so far as evidence

Enlightens one more darkness.   You have known

All round you, all your days, men who are nothing—

Nothing, I mean, so far as time tells yet

Of any other need it has of them

Than to make sextons hardy—but no less

Are to themselves incalculably something,

And therefore to be cherished.   God, you see,

Being sorry for them in their fashioning,

Indemnified them with a quaint esteem
Of self, and with illusions long as life.
You know them well, and you have smiled at them;
And they, in their serenity, may have had
Their time to smile at you.   Blessed are they
That see themselves for what they never were
Or were to be, and are, for their defect,
At ease with mirrors and the dim remarks
That pass their tranquil ears."


                    "Come, come," said I;
"There may be names in your compendium
That we are not yet all on fire for shouting.
Skin most of us of our mediocrity,
We should have nothing then that we could scratch.
The picture smarts.   Cover it, if you please,
And do so rather gently.   Now for Norcross."


Ferguson closed his eyes in resignation,
While a dead sigh came out of him.   "Good God!"
He said, and said it only half aloud,
As if he knew no longer now, nor cared,

If one were there to listen: "Have I said nothing—
Nothing at all—of Norcross? Do you mean
To patronize him till his name becomes
A toy made out of letters? If a name
Is all you need, arrange an honest column
Of all the people you have ever known
That you have never liked. You'll have enough;
And you'll have mine, moreover. No, not yet.
If I assume too many privileges,
I pay, and I alone, for their assumption;
By which, if I assume a darker knowledge
Of Norcross than another, let the weight
Of my injustice aggravate the load
That is not on your shoulders. When I came
To know this fellow Norcross in his house,
I found him as I found him in the street
No more, no less; indifferent, but no bettter.
'Worse' were not quite the word: he was not bad;
He was not . . . well, he was not anything.
Has your invention ever entertained
The picture of a dusty worm so dry
That even the early bird would shake his head
And fly on farther for another breakfast?"

"But why forget the fortune of the worm,"
I said, "if in the dryness you deplore
Salvation centred and endured?  Your Norcross
May have been one for many to have envied."

"Salvation?  Fortune?  Would the worm say that?
He might; and therefore I dismiss the worm
With all dry things but one.  Figures away,
Do you begin to see this man a little?
Do you begin to see him in the air,
With all the vacant horrors of his outline
For you to fill with more than it will hold?
If so, you needn't crown yourself at once
With epic laurel if you seem to fill it.
Horrors, I say, for in the fires and forks
Of a new hell—if one were not enough—
I doubt if a new horror would have held him
With a malignant ingenuity
More to be feared than his before he died.
You smile, as if in doubt.  Well, smile again.
Now come into his house, along with me:
The four square sombre things that you see first
Around you are four walls that go as high

As to the ceiling.  Norcross knew them well,
And he knew others like them.  Fasten to that
With all the claws of your intelligence;
And hold the man before you in his house
As if he were a white rat in a box,
And one that knew himself to be no other.
I tell you twice that he knew all about it,
That you may not forget the worst of all
Our tragedies begin with what we know.
Could Norcross only not have known, I wonder
How many would have blessed and envied him!
Could he have had the usual eye for spots
On others, and for none upon himself,
I smile to ponder on the carriages
That might as well as not have clogged the town
In honor of his end.  For there was gold,
You see, though all he needed was a little,
And what he gave said nothing of who gave it.
He would have given it all if in return
There might have been a more sufficient face
To greet him when he shaved.  Though you insist
It is the dower, and always, of our degree
Not to be cursed with such invidious insight.

Remember that you stand, you and your fancy,
Now in his house; and since we are together,
See for yourself and tell me what you see.
Tell me the best you see.  Make a slight noise
Of recognition when you find a book
That you would not as lief read upside down
As otherwise, for example.  If there you fail,
Observe the walls and lead me to the place
Where you are led.  If there you meet a picture
That holds you near it for a longer time
Than you are sorry, you may call it yours,
And hang it in the dark of your remembrance,
Where Norcross never sees.  How can he see
That has no eyes to see?  And as for music,
He paid with empty wonder for the pangs
Of his infrequent forced endurance of it;
And having had no pleasure, paid no more
For needless immolation, or for the sight
Of those who heard what he was never to hear.
To see them listening was itself enough
To make him suffer; and to watch worn eyes,
On other days, of strangers who forgot
Their sorrows and their failures and themselves

Before a few mysterious odds and ends
Of marble carted from the Parthenon—
And all for seeing what he was never to see,
Because it was alive and he was dead—
Here was a wonder that was more profound
Than any that was in fiddles and brass horns.

"He knew, and in his knowledge there was death.
He knew there was a region all around him
That lay outside man's havoc and affairs,
And yet was not all hostile to their tumult,
Where poets would have served and honored him,
And saved him, had there been anything to save.
But there was nothing, and his tethered range
Was only a small desert.  Kings of song
Are not for thrones in deserts.  Towers of sound
And flowers of sense are but a waste of heaven
Where there is none to know them from the rocks
And sand-grass of his own monotony
That makes earth less than earth.  He could see that,
And he could see no more.  The captured light
That may have been or not, for all he cared,
The song that is in sculpture was not his,

But only, to his God-forgotten eyes,
One more immortal nonsense in a world
Where all was mortal, or had best be so,
And so be done with. 'Art,' he would have said,
'Is not life, and must therefore be a lie;'
And with a few profundities like that
He would have controverted and dismissed
The benefit of the Greeks. He had heard of them,
As he had heard of his aspiring soul—
Never to the perceptible advantage,
In his esteem, of either. Faith, he said,
Or would have said if he had thought of it,
'Lives in the same house with Philosophy,
Where the two feed on scraps and are forlorn
As orphans after war.' He could see stars,
On a clear night, but he had not an eye
To see beyond them. He could hear spoken words,
But had no ear for silence when alone.
He could eat food of which he knew the savor,
But had no palate for the Bread of Life,
That human desperation, to his thinking,
Made famous long ago, having no other.
Now do you see? Do you begin to see?"

I told him that I did begin to see;
And I was nearer than I should have been
To laughing at his malign inclusiveness,
When I considered that, with all our speed,
We are not laughing yet at funerals.
I see him now as I could see him then,
And I see now that it was good for me,
As it was good for him, that I was quiet;
For Time's eye was on Ferguson, and the shaft
Of its inquiring hesitancy had touched him,
Or so I chose to fancy more than once
Before he told of Norcross.  When the word
Of his release (he would have called it so)
Made half an inch of news, there were no tears
That are recorded.  Women there may have been
To wish him back, though I should say, not knowing,
The few there were to mourn were not for love,
And were not lovely.  Nothing of them, at least,
Was in the meagre legend that I gathered
Years after, when a chance of travel took me
So near the region of his nativity
That a few miles of leisure brought me there;
For there I found a friendly citizen

Who led me to his house among the trees
That were above a railroad and a river.
Square as a box and chillier than a tomb
It was indeed, to look at or to live in—
All which had I been told.  "Ferguson died,"
The stranger said, "and then there was an auction.
I live here, but I've never yet been warm.
Remember him?  Yes, I remember him.
I knew him—as a man may know a tree—
For twenty years.  He may have held himself
A little high when he was here, but now . . .
Yes, I remember Ferguson.  Oh, yes."
Others, I found, remembered Ferguson,
But none of them had heard of Tasker Norcross.

# A SONG AT SHANNON'S

Two men came out of Shannon's, having known
The faces of each other for as long
As they had listened there to an old song,
Sung thinly in a wastrel monotone
By some unhappy night-bird, who had flown
Too many times and with a wing too strong
To save himself, and so done heavy wrong
To more frail elements than his alone.

Slowly away they went, leaving behind
More light than was before them.  Neither met
The other's eyes again or said a word.
Each to his loneliness or to his kind,
Went his own way, and with his own regret,
Not knowing what the other may have heard.

# SOUVENIR

A vanished house that for an hour I knew
By some forgotten chance when I was young
Had once a glimmering window overhung
With honeysuckle wet with evening dew.
Along the path tall dusky dahlias grew,
And shadowy hydrangeas reached and swung
Ferociously; and over me, among
The moths and mysteries, a blurred bat flew.

Somewhere within there were dim presences
Of days that hovered and of years gone by.
I waited, and between their silences
There was an evanescent faded noise;
And though a child, I knew it was the voice
Of one whose occupation was to die.

# DISCOVERY

We told of him as one who should have soared
And seen for us the devastating light
Whereof there is not either day or night,
And shared with us the glamour of the Word
That fell once upon Amos to record
For men at ease in Zion, when the sight
Of ills obscured aggrieved him and the might
Of Hamath was a warning of the Lord.

Assured somehow that he would make us wise,
Our pleasure was to wait; and our surprise
Was hard when we confessed the dry return
Of his regret.  For we were still to learn
That earth has not a school where we may go
For wisdom, or for more than we may know.

# FIRELIGHT

Ten years together without yet a cloud,
They seek each other's eyes at intervals
Of gratefulness to firelight and four walls
For love's obliteration of the crowd.
Serenely and perennially endowed
And bowered as few may be, their joy recalls
No snake, no sword; and over them there falls
The blessing of what neither says aloud.

Wiser for silence, they were not so glad
Were she to read the graven tale of lines
On the wan face of one somewhere alone;
Nor were they more content could he have had
Her thoughts a moment since of one who shines
Apart, and would be hers if he had known.

# THE NEW TENANTS

The day was here when it was his to know
How fared the barriers he had built between
His triumph and his enemies unseen,
For them to undermine and overthrow;
And it was his no longer to forego
The sight of them, insidious and serene,
Where they were delving always and had been
Left always to be vicious and to grow.

And there were the new tenants who had come,
By doors that were left open unawares,
Into his house, and were so much at home
There now that he would hardly have to guess,
By the slow guile of their vindictiveness,
What ultimate insolence would soon be theirs.

# INFERENTIAL

Although I saw before me there the face
Of one whom I had honored among men
The least, and on regarding him again
Would not have had him in another place,
He fitted with an unfamiliar grace
The coffin where I could not see him then
As I had seen him and appraised him when
I deemed him unessential to the race.

For there was more of him than what I saw,
And there was on me more than the old awe
That is the common genius of the dead.
I might as well have heard him: "Never mind;
If some of us were not so far behind,
The rest of us were not so far ahead."

# THE RAT

As often as he let himself be seen
We pitied him, or scorned him, or deplored
The inscrutable profusion of the Lord
Who shaped as one of us a thing so mean—
Who made him human when he might have been
A rat, and so been wholly in accord
With any other creature we abhorred
As always useless and not always clean.

Now he is hiding all alone somewhere,
And in a final hole not ready then;
For now he is among those over there
Who are not coming back to us again.
And we who do the fiction of our share
Say less of rats and rather more of men.

# RAHEL TO VARNHAGEN

Note.—Rahel Robert and Varnhagen von Ense were married, after
many protestations on her part, in 1814. The marriage—so far as he
was concerned at any rate—appears to have been satisfactory.

Now you have read them all; or if not all,

As many as in all conscience I should fancy

To be enough. There are no more of them—

Or none to burn your sleep, or to bring dreams

Of devils. If these are not sufficient, surely

You are a strange young man. I might live on

Alone, and for another forty years,

Or not quite forty,—are you happier now?—

Always to ask if there prevailed elsewhere

Another like yourself that would have held

These aged hands as long as you have held them,

Not once observing, for all I can see,

How they are like your mother's. Well, you have read

His letters now, and you have heard me say

That in them are the cinders of a passion

That was my life; and you have not yet broken

Your way out of my house, out of my sight,—

Into the street. You are a strange young man.

I know as much as that of you, for certain;

And I'm already praying, for your sake,
That you be not too strange.   Too much of that
May lead you bye and bye through gloomy lanes
To a sad wilderness, where one may grope
Alone, and always, or until he feels
Ferocious and invisible animals
That wait for men and eat them in the dark.
Why do you sit there on the floor so long,
Smiling at me while I try to be solemn?
Do you not hear it said for your salvation,
When I say truth?   Are you, at four and twenty,
So little deceived in us that you interpret
The humor of a woman to be noticed
As her choice between you and Acheron?
Are you so unscathed yet as to infer
That if a woman worries when a man,
Or a man-child, has wet shoes on his feet
She may as well commemorate with ashes
The last eclipse of her tranquillity?
If you look up at me and blink again,
I shall not have to make you tell me lies
To know the letters you have not been reading.
I see now that I may have had for nothing

A most unpleasant shivering in my conscience
When I laid open for your contemplation
The wealth of my worn casket.  If I did,
The fault was not yours wholly.  Search again
This wreckage we may call for sport a face,
And you may chance upon the price of havoc
That I have paid for a few sorry stones
That shine and have no light—yet once were stars,
And sparkled on a crown.  Little and weak
They seem; and they are cold, I fear, for you.
But they that once were fire for me may not
Be cold again for me until I die;
And only God knows if they may be then.
There is a love that ceases to be love
In being ourselves.  How, then, are we to lose it?
You that are sure that you know everything
There is to know of love, answer me that.
Well? . . . You are not even interested.

Once on a far off time when I was young,
I felt with your assurance, and all through me,
That I had undergone the last and worst
Of love's inventions.  There was a boy who brought

The sun with him and woke me up with it,
And that was every morning; every night
I tried to dream of him, but never could,
More than I might have seen in Adam's eyes
Their fond uncertainty when Eve began
The play that all her tireless progeny
Are not yet weary of. One scene of it
Was brief, but was eternal while it lasted;
And that was while I was the happiest
Of an imaginary six or seven,
Somewhere in history but not on earth,
For whom the sky had shaken and let stars
Rain down like diamonds. Then there were clouds,
And a sad end of diamonds; whereupon
Despair came, like a blast that would have brought
Tears to the eyes of all the bears in Finland,
And love was done. That was how much I knew.
Poor little wretch! I wonder where he is
This afternoon. Out of this rain, I hope.

At last, when I had seen so many days
Dressed all alike, and in their marching order,
Go by me that I would not always count them,

One stopped—shattering the whole file of Time,
Or so it seemed; and when I looked again,
There was a man. He struck once with his eyes,
And then there was a woman. I, who had come
To wisdom, or to vision, or what you like,
By the old hidden road that has no name,—
I, who was used to seeing without flying
So much that others fly from without seeing,
Still looked, and was afraid, and looked again.
And after that, when I had read the story
Told in his eyes, and felt within my heart
The bleeding wound of their necessity,
I knew the fear was his. If I had failed him
And flown away from him, I should have lost
Ingloriously my wings in scrambling back,
And found them arms again. If he had struck me
Not only with his eyes but with his hands,
I might have pitied him and hated love,
And then gone mad. I, who have been so strong—
Why don't you laugh?—might even have done all that.
I, who have learned so much, and said so much,
And had the commendations of the great
For one who rules herself—why don't you cry?—

And own a certain small authority
Among the blind, who see no more than ever,
But like my voice —I would have tossed it all
To Tophet for one man; and he was jealous.
I would have wound a snake around my neck
And then have let it bite me till I died,
If my so doing would have made me sure
That one man might have lived; and he was jealous.
I would have driven these hands into a cage
That held a thousand scorpions, and crushed them,
If only by so poisonous a trial
I could have crushed his doubt.   I would have wrung
My living blood with mediaeval engines
Out of my screaming flesh, if only that
Would have made one man sure.   I would have paid
For him the tiresome price of body and soul,
And let the lash of a tongue-weary town
Fall as it might upon my blistered name;
And while it fell I could have laughed at it,
Knowing that he had found out finally
Where the wrong was.   But there was evil in him
That would have made no more of his possession
Than confirmation of another fault;

And there was honor—if you call it honor
That hoods itself with doubt and wears a crown
Of lead that might as well be gold and fire.
Give it as heavy or as light a name
As any there is that fits.  I see myself
Without the power to swear to this or that
That I might be if he had been without it.
Whatever I might have been that I was not,
It only happened that it wasn't so.
Meanwhile, you might seem to be listening:
If you forget yourself and go to sleep,
My treasure, I shall not say this again.
Look up once more into my poor old face,
Where you see beauty, or the Lord knows what,
And say to me aloud what else there is
That ruins in it that you most admire.

No, there was never anything like that;
Nature has never fastened such a mask
Of radiant and impenetrable merit
On any woman as you say there is
On this one.  Not a mask?  I thank you, sir,
But you see more with your determination,

I fear, than with your prudence or your conscience;
And you have never met me with my eyes
In all the mirrors I've made faces at.
No, I shall never call you strange again:
You are the young and inconvincible
Epitome of all blind men since Adam.
May the blind lead the blind, if that be so?
And we shall need no mirrors?  You are saying
What most I feared you might.  But if the blind,
Or one of them, be not so fortunate
As to put out the eyes of recollection,
She might at last, without her meaning it,
Lead on the other, without his knowing it,
Until the two of them should lose themselves
Among dead craters in a lava-field
As empty as a desert on the moon.
I am not speaking in a theatre,
But in a room so real and so familiar
That sometimes I would wreck it.  Then I pause,
Remembering there is a King in Weimar—
A monarch, and a poet, and a shepherd
Of all who are astray and are outside
The realm where they should rule.  I think of him,

And save the furniture; I think of you,
And am forlorn, finding in you the one
To lavish aspirations and illusions
Upon a faded and forsaken house
Where love, being locked alone, was nigh to burning
House and himself together.  Yes, you are strange,
To see in such an injured architecture
Room for new love to live in.  Are you laughing?
No?  Well, you are not crying, as you should be.
Tears, even if they told only gratitude
For your escape, and had no other story,
Were surely more becoming than a smile
For my unwomanly straightforwardness
In seeing for you, through my close gate of years
Your forty ways to freedom.  Why do you smile?
And while I'm trembling at my faith in you
In giving you to read this book of danger
That only one man living might have written—
These letters, which have been a part of me
So long that you may read them all again
As often as you look into my face,
And hear them when I speak to you, and feel them
Whenever you have to touch me with your hand,—

Why are you so unwilling to be spared?
Why do you still believe in me?   But no,
I'll find another way to ask you that.
I wonder if there is another way
That says it better, and means anything.
There is no other way that could be worse?
I was not asking you; it was myself
Alone that I was asking.   Why do I dip
For lies, when there is nothing in my well
But shining truth, you say?   How do you know?
Truth has a lonely life down where she lives;
And many a time, when she comes up to breathe,
She sinks before we seize her, and makes ripples.
Possibly you may know no more of me
Than a few ripples; and they may soon be gone,
Leaving you then with all my shining truth
Drowned in a shining water; and when you look
You may not see me there, but something else
That never was a woman—being yourself.
You say to me my truth is past all drowning,
And safe with you for ever?   You know all that?
How do you know all that, and who has told you?
You know so much that I'm an atom frightened

Because you know so little.   And what is this?
You know the luxury there is in haunting
The blasted thoroughfares of disillusion—
If that's your name for them—with only ghosts
For company?   You know that when a woman
Is blessed, or cursed, with a divine impatience
(Another name of yours for a bad temper)
She must have one at hand on whom to wreak it
(That's what you mean, whatever the turn you give it),
Sure of a kindred sympathy, and thereby
Effect a mutual calm?   You know that wisdom,
Given in vain to make a food for those
Who are without it, will be seen at last,
And even at last only by those who gave it,
As one or more of the forgotten crumbs
That others leave?   You know that men's applause
And women's envy savor so much of dust
That I go hungry, having at home no fare
But the same changeless bread that I may swallow
Only with tears and prayers?   Who told you that?
You know that if I read, and read alone,
Too many books that no men yet have written,
I may go blind, or worse?   You know yourself,

Of all insistent and insidious creatures,
To be the one to save me, and to guard
For me their flaming language?  And you know
That if I give much headway to the whim
That's in me never to be quite sure that even
Through all those years of storm and fire I waited
For this one rainy day, I may go on,
And on, and on alone, through smoke and ashes,
To a cold end?  You know so dismal much
As that about me? . . . Well, I believe you do。

# NIMMO

Since you remember Nimmo, and arrive
At such a false and florid and far drawn
Confusion of odd nonsense, I connive
No longer, though I may have led you on.

So much is told and heard and told again,
So many with his legend are engrossed,
That I, more sorry now than I was then,
May live on to be sorry for his ghost.

You knew him, and you must have known his eyes,—
How deep they were, and what a velvet light
Came out of them when anger or surprise,
Or laughter, or Francesca, made them bright.

No, you will not forget such eyes, I think,—
And you say nothing of them.  Very well.
I wonder if all history's worth a wink,
Sometimes, or if my tale be one to tell.

For they began to lose their velvet light;
Their fire grew dead without and small within;

And many of you deplored the needless fight
That somewhere in the dark there must have been.


All fights are needless, when they're not our own,
But Nimmo and Francesca never fought.
Remember that; and when you are alone,
Remember me—and think what I have thought.


Now, mind you, I say nothing of what was,
Or never was, or could or could not be:
Bring not suspicion's candle to the glass
That mirrors a friend's face to memory.


Of what you see, see all,—but see no more;
For what I show you here will not be there.
The devil has had his way with paint before,
And he's an artist,—and you needn't stare.


There was a painter and he painted well:
He'd paint you Daniel in the lion's den,
Beelzebub, Elaine, or William Tell.
I'm coming back to Nimmo's eyes again.

The painter put the devil in those eyes,
Unless the devil did, and there he stayed;
And then the lady fled from paradise,
And there's your fact.   The lady was afraid.

She must have been afraid, or may have been,
Of evil in their velvet all the while;
But sure as I'm a sinner with a skin,
I'll trust the man as long as he can smile.

I trust him who can smile and then may live
In my heart's house, where Nimmo is to-day.
God knows if I have more than men forgive
To tell him; but I played, and I shall pay.

I knew him then, and if I know him yet,
I know in him, defeated and estranged,
The calm of men forbidden to forget
The calm of women who have loved and changed.

But there are ways that are beyond our ways,
Or he would not be calm and she be mute,
As one by one their lost and empty days
Pass without even the warmth of a dispute.

God help us all when women think they see;
God save us when they do.  I'm fair; but though
I know him only as he looks to me,
I know him,—and I tell Francesca so.

And what of Nimmo?   Little would you ask
Of him, could you but see him as I can,
At his bewildered and unfruitful task
Of being what he was born to be—a man.

Better forget that I said anything
Of what your tortured memory may disclose;
I know him, and your worst remembering
Would count as much as nothing, I suppose.

Meanwhile, I trust him; and I know his way
Of trusting me, as always in his youth.
I'm painting here a better man, you say,
Than I, the painter; and you say the truth.

[111]

# PEACE ON EARTH

He took a frayed hat from his head,
And "Peace on Earth" was what he said.
"A morsel out of what you're worth,
And there we have it: Peace on Earth.
Not much, although a little more
Than what there was on earth before.
I'm as you see, I'm Ichabod,—
But never mind the ways I've trod;
I'm sober now, so help me God."


I could not pass the fellow by.
"Do you believe in God? " said I;
"And is there to be Peace on Earth? "


"To-night we celebrate the birth,"
He said, "of One who died for men;
The Son of God, we say.   What then?
Your God, or mine?   I'd make you laugh
Were I to tell you even half
That I have learned of mine to-day
Where yours would hardly seem to stay.

Could he but follow in and out
Some anthropoids I know about,
The God to whom you may have prayed
Might see a world he never made."

"Your words are flowing full," said I;
"But yet they give me no reply;
Your fountain might as well be dry."

"A wiser One than you, my friend,
Would wait and hear me to the end;
And for his eyes a light would shine
Through this unpleasant shell of mine
That in your fancy makes of me
A Christmas curiosity.
All right, I might be worse than that;
And you might now be lying flat;
I might have done it from behind,
And taken what there was to find.
Don't worry, for I'm not that kind.
'Do I believe in God?'  Is that
The price to-night of a new hat?
Has he commanded that his name

Be written everywhere the same?
Have all who live in every place
Identified his hidden face?
Who knows but he may like as well
My story as one you may tell?
And if he show me there be Peace
On Earth, as there be fields and trees
Outside a jail-yard, am I wrong
If now I sing him a new song?
Your world is in yourself, my friend,
For your endurance to the end;
And all the Peace there is on Earth
Is faith in what your world is worth,
And saying, without any lies,
Your world could not be otherwise."

"One might say that and then be shot,"
I told him; and he said: "Why not?"
I ceased, and gave him rather more
Than he was counting of my store.
"And since I have it, thanks to you,
Don't ask me what I mean to do,"
Said he.  "Believe that even I

Would rather tell the truth than lie—
On Christmas Eve.   No matter why."

His unshaved, educated face,
His inextinguishable grace,
And his hard smile, are with me still,
Deplore the vision as I will;
For whatsoever he be at,
So droll a derelict as that
Should have at least another hat.

# LATE SUMMER

## (ALCAICS)

Confused, he found her lavishing feminine
Gold upon clay, and found her inscrutable;
    And yet she smiled.  Why, then, should horrors
Be as they were, without end, her playthings?


And why were dead years hungrily telling her
Lies of the dead, who told them again to her?
    If now she knew, there might be kindness
Clamoring yet where a faith lay stifled.


A little faith in him, and the ruinous
Past would be for time to annihilate,
    And wash out, like a tide that washes
Out of the sand what a child has drawn there.


God, what a shining handful of happiness,
Made out of days and out of eternities,
    Were now the pulsing end of patience—
Could he but have what a ghost had stolen!

[116]

What was a man before him, or ten of them,
While he was here alive who could answer them,
    And in their teeth fling confirmations
Harder than agates against an egg-shell?

But now the man was dead, and would come again
Never, though she might honor ineffably
    The flimsy wraith of him she conjured
Out of a dream with his wand of absence.

And if the truth were now but a mummery,
Meriting pride's implacable irony,
    So much the worse for pride.   Moreover,
Save her or fail, there was conscience always.

Meanwhile, a few misgivings of innocence,
Imploring to be sheltered and credited,
    Were not amiss when she revealed them.
Whether she struggled or not, he saw them.

Also, he saw that while she was hearing him
Her eyes had more and more of the past in them;
    And while he told what cautious honor
Told him was all he had best be sure of,

He wondered once or twice, inadvertently,
Where shifting winds were driving his argosies,
　　　Long anchored and as long unladen,
Over the foam for the golden chances.

"If men were not for killing so carelessly,
And women were for wiser endurances,"
　　　He said, "we might have yet a world here
Fitter for Truth to be seen abroad in;

"If Truth were not so strange in her nakedness
And we were less forbidden to look at it,
　　　We might not have to look." He stared then
Down at the sand where the tide threw forward

Its cold, unconquered lines, that unceasingly
Foamed against hope, and fell. He was calm enough,
　　　Although he knew he might be silenced
Out of all calm; and the night was coming.

"I climb for you the peak of his infamy
That you may choose your fall if you cling to it.
　　　No more for me unless you say more.
All you have left of a dream defends you:

"The truth may be as evil an augury
As it was needful now for the two of us.
    We cannot have the dead between us.
Tell me to go, and I go."—She pondered:


"What you believe is right for the two of us
Makes it as right that you are not one of us.
    If this be needful truth you tell me,
Spare me, and let me have lies hereafter."


She gazed away where shadows were covering
The whole cold ocean's healing indifference.
    No ship was coming.  When the darkness
Fell, she was there, and alone, still gazing.

# AN EVANGELIST'S WIFE

"Why am I not myself these many days,
You ask?  And have you nothing more to ask?
I do you wrong?  I do not hear your praise
To God for giving you me to share your task?


"Jealous—of Her?  Because her cheeks are pink,
And she has eyes?  No, not if she had seven.
If you should only steal an hour to think,
Sometime, there might be less to be forgiven.


"No, you are never cruel.  If once or twice
I found you so, I could applaud and sing.
Jealous of—What?  You are not very wise.
Does not the good Book tell you anything?


"In David's time poor Michal had to go.
Jealous of God?  Well, if you like it so."

# THE OLD KING'S NEW JESTER

You that in vain would front the coming order
With eyes that meet forlornly what they must,
And only with a furtive recognition
See dust where there is dust,—
Be sure you like it always in your faces,
Obscuring your best graces,
Blinding your speech and sight,
Before you seek again your dusty places
Where the old wrong seems right.

Longer ago than cave-men had their changes
Our fathers may have slain a son or two,
Discouraging a further dialectic
Regarding what was new;
And after their unstudied admonition
Occasional contrition
For their old-fashioned ways
May have reduced their doubts, and in addition
Softened their final days.

Farther away than feet shall ever travel
Are the vague towers of our unbuilded State;

But there are mightier things than we to lead us,
That will not let us wait.
And we go on with none to tell us whether
Or not we've each a tether
Determining how fast or far we go;
And it is well, since we must go together,
That we are not to know.

If the old wrong and all its injured glamour
Haunts you by day and gives your night no peace,
You may as well, agreeably and serenely,
Give the new wrong its lease;
For should you nourish a too fervid yearning
For what is not returning,
The vicious and unfused ingredient
May give you qualms—and one or two concerning
The last of your content.

# LAZARUS

"No, Mary, there was nothing—not a word.
Nothing, and always nothing.  Go again
Yourself, and he may listen—or at least
Look up at you, and let you see his eyes.
I might as well have been the sound of rain,
A wind among the cedars, or a bird;
Or nothing.  Mary, make him look at you;
And even if he should say that we are nothing,
To know that you have heard him will be something.
And yet he loved us, and it was for love
The Master gave him back.  Why did he wait
So long before he came?  Why did he weep?
I thought he would be glad—and Lazarus—
To see us all again as he had left us—
All as it was, all as it was before."


Mary, who felt her sister's frightened arms
Like those of someone drowning who had seized her,
Fearing at last they were to fail and sink
Together in this fog-stricken sea of strangeness,
Fought sadly, with bereaved indignant eyes,

To find again the fading shores of home
That she had seen but now could see no longer.
Now she could only gaze into the twilight,
And in the dimness know that he was there,
Like someone that was not.  He who had been
Their brother, and was dead, now seemed alive
Only in death again—or worse than death;
For tombs at least, always until to-day,
Though sad were certain.  There was nothing certain
For man or God in such a day as this;
For there they were alone, and there was he—
Alone; and somewhere out of Bethany,
The Master—who had come to them so late,
Only for love of them and then so slowly,
And was for their sake hunted now by men
Who feared Him as they feared no other prey—
For the world's sake was hidden.  "Better the tomb
For Lazarus than life, if this be life,"
She thought; and then to Martha, "No, my dear,"
She said aloud; "not as it was before.
Nothing is ever as it was before,
Where Time has been.  Here there is more than Time;
And we that are so lonely and so far

From home, since he is with us here again,
Are farther now from him and from ourselves
Than we are from the stars.  He will not speak
Until the spirit that is in him speaks;
And we must wait for all we are to know,
Or even to learn that we are not to know.
Martha, we are too near to this for knowledge,
And that is why it is that we must wait.
Our friends are coming if we call for them,
And there are covers we'll put over him
To make him warmer.  We are too young, perhaps,
To say that we know better what is best
Than he.  We do not know how old he is.
If you remember what the Master said,
Try to believe that we need have no fear.
Let me, the selfish and the careless one,
Be housewife and a mother for to-night;
For I am not so fearful as you are,
And I was not so eager."


                    Martha sank
Down at her sister's feet and there sat watching
A flower that had a small familiar name

That was as old as memory, but was not
The name of what she saw now in its brief
And infinite mystery that so frightened her
That life became a terror.  Tears again
Flooded her eyes and overflowed.  "No, Mary,"
She murmured slowly, hating her own words
Before she heard them, "you are not so eager
To see our brother as we see him now;
Neither is he who gave him back to us.
I was to be the simple one, as always,
And this was all for me."  She stared again
Over among the trees where Lazarus,
Who seemed to be a man who was not there,
Might have been one more shadow among shadows,
If she had not remembered.  Then she felt
The cool calm hands of Mary on her face,
And shivered, wondering if such hands were real.


"The Master loved you as he loved us all,
Martha; and you are saying only things
That children say when they have had no sleep.
Try somehow now to rest a little while·

You know that I am here, and that our friends
Are coming if I call."

                    Martha at last
Arose, and went with Mary to the door,
Where they stood looking off at the same place,
And at the same shape that was always there
As if it would not ever move or speak,
And always would be there.  "Mary, go now,
Before the dark that will be coming hides him.
I am afraid of him out there alone,
Unless I see him; and I have forgotten
What sleep is.  Go now—make him look at you—
And I shall hear him if he stirs or whispers.
Go!—or I'll scream and bring all Bethany
To come and make him speak.  Make him say once
That he is glad, and God may say the rest.
Though He say I shall sleep, and sleep for ever,
I shall not care for that . . . Go!"

                              Mary, moving
Almost as if an angry child had pushed her,
Went forward a few steps; and having waited
As long as Martha's eyes would look at hers,

Went forward a few more, and a few more;
And so, until she came to Lazarus,
Who crouched with his face hidden in his hands,
Like one that had no face. Before she spoke,
Feeling her sister's eyes that were behind her
As if the door where Martha stood were now
As far from her as Egypt, Mary turned
Once more to see that she was there. Then, softly,
Fearing him not so much as wondering
What his first word might be, said, "Lazarus,
Forgive us if we seemed afraid of you;"
And having spoken, pitied her poor speech
That had so little seeming gladness in it,
So little comfort, and so little love.

There was no sign from him that he had heard,
Or that he knew that she was there, or cared
Whether she spoke to him again or died
There at his feet. "We love you, Lazarus,
And we are not afraid. The Master said
We need not be afraid. Will you not say
To me that you are glad? Look, Lazarus!
Look at my face, and see me. This is Mary."

She found his hands and held them.  They were cool,
Like hers, but they were not so calm as hers.
Through the white robes in which his friends had wrapped him
When he had groped out of that awful sleep,
She felt him trembling and she was afraid.
At last he sighed; and she prayed hungrily
To God that she might hear again the voice
Of Lazarus, whose hands were giving her now
The recognition of a living pressure
That was almost a language.  When he spoke,
Only one word that she had waited for
Came from his lips, and that word was her name.

"I heard them saying, Mary, that he wept
Before I woke."  The words were low and shaken,
Yet Mary knew that he who uttered them
Was Lazarus; and that would be enough
Until there should be more . . . "Who made him come,
That he should weep for me? . . . Was it you, Mary?"
The questions held in his incredulous eyes
Were more than she would see.  She looked away;
But she had felt them and should feel for ever,
She thought, their cold and lonely desperation

That had the bitterness of all cold things
That were not cruel. "I should have wept," he said,
"If I had been the Master. . . ."

Now she could feel
His hands above her hair—the same black hair
That once he made a jest of, praising it,
While Martha's busy eyes had left their work
To flash with laughing envy. Nothing of that
Was to be theirs again; and such a thought
Was like the flying by of a quick bird
Seen through a shadowy doorway in the twilight.
For now she felt his hands upon her head,
Like weights of kindness: "I forgive you, Mary. . . .
You did not know—Martha could not have known—
Only the Master knew. . . . Where is he now?
Yes, I remember. They came after him.
May the good God forgive him. . . . I forgive him.
I must; and I may know only from him
The burden of all this. . . . Martha was here—
But I was not yet here. She was afraid. . . .
Why did he do it, Mary? Was it—you?
Was it for you? . . . Where are the friends I saw?

Yes, I remember.  They all went away.
I made them go away. . . .  Where is he now? . . .
What do I see down there?   Do I see Martha—
Down  by  the  door? . . . I  must  have  time  for  this."


Lazarus looked about him fearfully,
And then again at Mary, who discovered
Awakening apprehension in his eyes,
And shivered at his feet.   All she had feared
Was here; and only in the slow reproach
Of his forgiveness lived his gratitude.
Why had he asked if it was all for her
That he was here?   And what had Martha meant?
Why had the Master waited?   What was coming
To Lazarus, and to them, that had not come?
What had the Master seen before he came,
That he had come so late?


                    "Where is he, Mary?"
Lazarus asked again.   "Where did he go?"
Once more he gazed about him, and once more
At Mary for an answer.   "Have they found him?
Or did he go away because he wished

Never to look into my eyes again? . . .
That, I could understand. . . . Where is he, Mary?"

"I do not know," she said. "Yet in my heart
I know that he is living, as you are living—
Living, and here. He is not far from us.
He will come back to us and find us all—
Lazarus, Martha, Mary—everything—
All as it was before. Martha said that.
And he said we were not to be afraid."
Lazarus closed his eyes while on his face
A tortured adumbration of a smile
Flickered an instant. "All as it was before,"
He murmured wearily. "Martha said that;
And he said you were not to be afraid . . .
Not you . . . Not you . . . Why should you be afraid?
Give all your little fears, and Martha's with them,
To me; and I will add them unto mine,
Like a few rain-drops to Gennesaret."

"If you had frightened me in other ways,
Not willing it," Mary said, "I should have known
You still for Lazarus. But who is this?

Tell me again that you are Lazarus;
And tell me if the Master gave to you
No sign of a new joy that shall be coming
To this house that he loved.   Are you afraid?
Are you afraid, who have felt everything—
And seen . . .?"

                    But Lazarus only shook his head,
Staring with his bewildered shining eyes
Hard into Mary's face.   "I do not know,
Mary," he said, and after a long time.
"When I came back, I knew the Master's eyes
Were looking into mine.   I looked at his,
And there was more in them than I could see.
At first I could see nothing but his eyes;
Nothing else anywhere was to be seen—
Only his eyes.   And they looked into mine—
Long into mine, Mary, as if he knew."


Mary began to be afraid of words
As she had never been afraid before
Of loneliness or darkness, or of death,
But now she must have more of them or die:

"He cannot know that there is worse than death,"
She said.  "And you . . ."

                              "Yes, there is worse than death."
Said Lazarus; "and that was what he knew;
And that is what it was that I could see
This morning in his eyes.  I was afraid,
But not as you are.  There is worse than death,
Mary; and there is nothing that is good
For you in dying while you are still here.
Mary, never go back to that again.
You would not hear me if I told you more,
For I should say it only in a language
That you are not to learn by going back.
To be a child again is to go forward—
And that is much to know.  Many grow old,
And fade, and go away, not knowing how much
That is to know.  Mary, the night is coming,
And there will soon be darkness all around you.
Let us go down where Martha waits for us,
And let there be light shining in this house."

He rose, but Mary would not let him go:
"Martha, when she came back from here, said only

That she heard nothing. And have you no more
For Mary now than you had then for Martha?
Is Nothing, Lazarus, all you have for me?
Was Nothing all you found where you have been?
If that be so, what is there worse than that—
Or better—if that be so? And why should you,
With even our love, go the same dark road over?"

"I could not answer that, if that were so,"
Said Lazarus,—"not even if I were God.
Why should He care whether I came or stayed,
If that were so? Why should the Master weep—
For me, or for the world,—or save himself
Longer for nothing? And if that were so,
Why should a few years' more mortality
Make him a fugitive where flight were needless,
Had he but held his peace and given his nod
To an old Law that would be new as any?
I cannot say the answer to all that;
Though I may say that he is not afraid,
And that it is not for the joy there is
In serving an eternal Ignorance
Of our futility that he is here.

Is that what you and Martha mean by Nothing?
Is that what you are fearing? If that be so,
There are more weeds than lentils in your garden.
And one whose weeds are laughing at his harvest
May as well have no garden; for not there
Shall he be gleaning the few bits and orts
Of life that are to save him. For my part,
I am again with you, here among shadows
That will not always be so dark as this;
Though now I see there's yet an evil in me
That made me let you be afraid of me.
No, I was not afraid—not even of life.
I thought I was . . . I must have time for this;
And all the time there is will not be long.
I cannot tell you what the Master saw
This morning in my eyes. I do not know.
I cannot yet say how far I have gone,
Or why it is that I am here again,
Or where the old road leads. I do not know.
I know that when I did come back, I saw
His eyes again among the trees and faces—
Only his eyes; and they looked into mine—
Long into mine—long, long, as if he knew."

# DIONYSUS IN DOUBT

## A BOOK OF POEMS

## (1925)

*To*
*Craven Longstroth Betts*

# DIONYSUS IN DOUBT

From earth as far away
As night from day,
Or sleep from waking,
Somewhere a dawn like none
Before was breaking.
For long there was no sight or sound
Of any other one
Than I that was alive on that strange ground,
When surely and ineffably aware
That something else was there,
I turned and saw before me, ivy-crowned,
Flame-born of Zeus and of a burning mother,
One of the wasteful gods that will be found
Though variously renowned,
Commensurable only with another.
And had he not been what he was—
Had he been one to live and have his day
Like us, who come and go away,—

My fancy might have made as if to see
Within his deathless eyes
A weariness, an incredulity,
And a benign surprise,
When over them would slowly pass,
Thinly and intermittently,
The filmy cloud of a cold augury.


"And what is this that we have here below?"
He said; whereat his eyes began to shine
As with a humor that was not for man
To fathom: "Will you tell me, if you can?
For you should know it well—
If not the story there may be to tell
Of a complacent yet impatient folk,
Anticipating and somewhat at ease
Already with millennial ecstasies
Of much too much at once.  You know
All that, and—even so."
As if a languid shrug would say the rest,
And say it best,
He paused, inquiringly;
Then with a downward finger made me look

Till I made out to see
A place that was no other land than mine.
"How long must you be waiting for a sign—
All you down there?" said he.

Having no converse with a god before,
Humility forbore
Too brisk an estimate; whereat he smiled,
And partly frowned.  "Where man remains a child,
The days are always longer than they are,
And there are more of them than are to be
As they have been.  All which is true," said he,
"Of an inflexible and hasty nation
That sees already done
Rather too much that has not yet begun.
I mention them that are so confident
In their abrupt and arbitrary ways
Of capturing and harnessing salvation
With nets and ropes of words that never meant
Before so little as in these tiresome days
Of tireless legislation;
Also I marvel at a land like yours,
Where predatory love

In freedom's name invades the last alcove;
And I foresee a reckoning, perforce,
That you, not eager to see far
From where your toys and trumpets are,
Make nothing of.

"Wherefore your freedom, given a time to pause,
Vindictively and unbecomingly
Becomes a prodigy for men to fear—
Or so she looks to me.
Appraising her from here,
I make of her an insecure delight
For man's prolonged abode,
And the wrong thing for him to meet at night
On a wrong road.
No wonder there are many of you perplexed
At her deceiving singularities,
And hazarding your fancy on the next
Of her oblique appearances;
Albeit as always you may only gape
And smile at her uncertain face and shape,
And thereby be indifferently amused—
Recovering too late your derelictions,

To find your tardy maledictions
All outlawed and refused.


"Freedom, familiar and at ease meanwhile
With your perennial smile,
Goes on with her old guile:
Having enjoined your conscience and your diet,
She spreads again her claws,
Preparatory, one infers,
From energy like hers,
For the infliction of more liberty;
And reckless of who reads them or desires them,
Regardless of who heeds them or requires them,
Fearful of someone left who might be quiet,
She clamps again her jaws
And makes a few more laws;
And you, you millions, or as many of you
As have not your herd-servitude in check,
Conspire somehow by law to wring the neck
Of nature, not seeing how large a neck it is
That your beneficent severities
Would humble and subdue—
To moronize the million for the few.

Oblivious of the many-venomed ways

Attendant on their failing who should fail,

By soporific tyranny misled

Into a specious maze

Where vermin unsupposable are bred,

You may not see a sign of the snake's tail

Whereon you are to tread."


With that he shook his head

As with a questioning, I thought,

Of his onslaught

Upon a fervid if inadequate

Insistence of an adolescent giant

To hang itself, if possible, defiant

Alike of too much weight

And of an ill-spun rope.

In weakness indirectly there was hope

For an unransomed kidnapped juvenile

Miscalled Democracy.

He met my divination with a smile

Of Heliconian serenity,

And soon resumed

His utterance as to one for faith entombed:

"Yes, there is hope where you believe it is;
Also intelligence is hidden there—
Much as a tree's unguessed immensities
Are hidden in a seed.
But more than both
Of these that are so excellent,
And so long in arriving,
Hypocrisy, timidity, and sloth
Are there and are all thriving.
Yes, they are there indeed:
I see them and assay their qualities;
Not many of them are fair,
Nor any of them so rare
As to be known with more astonishment
Than are the most of man's idolatries,
Wherein you find him almost everywhere
Perniciously at prayer
For consummation and a furtherance
Of his benevolent ingrained repression
Of the next man's possession.
All which has no illusion, or surprise,
Or pleasure for my eyes.
If I withhold from yours the benefit

Of seeing with mine within and round about
Your region here below,
Whereto your steps will soon again be going—
Sometimes it may be better not to know
Than to be stoned for knowing."

Here my remonstrance with a smooth rebuff
Was laughed at once aside:
"All that is coming will come soon enough,"
He said, "and it will be no balm for pride;
And one forlorn prediction will achieve
No remedy or reprieve.
There are some fiery letters never learned
Till children who are reading them are burned
Before they are aware of any fire.
Remember that, all you that would aspire,
Unsinged and all alone,
To the unseen and the discredited,
And to the best for you unknown.
If I, meanwhile,
Appropriate the salvage of a smile,
You may take heart, and cease to look ahead.
Fatuities ripe for dying will be dead

Sometime, imaginably;
Wherefore, to be the more commendable
To my esteem, you may as well
Invent for me the best essential name
For him that with one hand puts out
The flame that warms a fluctuating brother,
And meritoriously with the other
Pours unpermitted oil upon his own.
Well, if you falter, give yourself no pain
To say aloud the undiscovered word
That I consign to silence and let be.
The gods will on occasion delve in vain
For nomenclature more profound,
And more absurd,
Than gods have ever heard
For their assurance that a cube is round.
But your proficient idiom, not averse
To nonsense or a nullifying curse,
Will pray for you till you forget
That when a sphere is hammered square
All that was hammered is still there;
Also that Humbug is no less
Himself in his best dress.

[ 23 ]

I'm watching him, yet I see one that's worse

For your concern than he:

Delinquent in two-fold apostasy,

This other's doings

Are like the tepid wooings

Of him who jilts the woman of his choice

Because another with a shrewder voice,

And with some innuendoes of a past,

Inveigles him until she has him fast,

Innocuous and amenable at last.


Wherever the dissension or the danger

Or the distrust may be,

All you that for timidity

Or for expediency capitulate,

Are negative in yourselves and in the state;

Yet there are worse for you to see,

As everywhere you may remark:

Some animals, if you see them in a manger

And do not hear them bark,

Are silent not for any watch they keep,

Nor yet for love of whatso comes to feed,

But pleasantly and ineffectually

Are silent there because they are asleep.
There are too many sleepers in your land,
And in too many places
Defeat, indifference, and forsworn command
Are like a mask upon too many faces.
There are too many who stand
Erect and always amiable in error,
And always in accommodating terror
Before the glimmering imminence
Of too insistent a sincerity;
Too many are recommended not to see,
Or loudly to suggest,
That opulence, compromise, and lethargy
Together are not the bravest or the best
Among the imaginable remedies
For a young world's unrest;
Too many are not at all distressed
Or noticeably ill at ease
With nature's inner counsel when it means
That if a drowsy wisdom blinks and leans
Too much on legioned innocence
Armed only with a large mistake,
Something is due to shake;

Too many among you, having learned
Expediently how not to think,
Will close your mouths where I'm concerned—
Except to drink."

Over his face once more
There passed a cloud that I had seen before;
But soon the frowning eyes were cleared,
And with another smile
Were fixed on mine a while:
"Sometimes I wonder what machine
Your innocence will employ,"
He said at length,
"When all are niched and ticketed and all
Are standardized and unexceptional,
To perpetrate complacency and joy
Of uniform size and strength;
Sometimes I ponder whether you have seen,
Or contemplated over much down there,
The treacherous way that you are now pursuing,
Or by just what immeasurable expense
Of unexplained omnipotence
You are to make it lead you anywhere

Than to the wonder of a sick despair

That waits upon a gullible undoing.

So much of the insoluble

As that is not for me to tell.

For all I know,

An ultimate uniformity enthroned

May trim your vision very well;

And the poor cringing self, disowned,

May call it freedom and efficiency.

Others would somewhat rather call it hell,

And rather not be quite so free

To blend themselves with mediocrity.

How then your follies are to show

The vengeance they are now concealing,—

What your conformity may then resign

To perils more to fear them mine,—

How safe an average then may be decided

And what last prize divided,

Are manifestly not for my revealing.

If you are still too drowsy now to keep

The vigil of at least a glance

On that which reinforced intolerance

May next of yours be stealing,
From now to then you had all better sleep.


"In legend once there was a perfect bed,
Which your new freedom has inherited.
By virtue of much stretching and some cleaving,
All bound upon it were conformably
Certificated there for the receiving
Of its whole warmth and hospitality—
One man no longer than another
And every man thereby a brother.
If you misprize my word,
You may look down again from here to see
How eagerly the prisoners will agree
In liberty's illimitable name,
All to be made the same.
If proof inhibits your belief
My observation therein may have erred;
And there may still be no mistake
Of their disparities, or in the status
Of so gratuitous an apparatus
Among contrivances designed
To make men sorry for their kind,

[ 28 ]

Proving at last a laughter and a grief
To sting them like a snake.

"There are so many stories about snakes
In the perilous book of truth as it is written,
That all who will not read
Or in appearance will not heed—
Though dimly and unwillingly they must—
An inward venom of a slow mistrust,
May never tell you by a word or look
By what less pleasant serpent they are bitten
Than any in the book.
Happy as children eating worm-ripe fruit,
Praising the obvious for the absolute,
They see an end of that which has no end
Of their devising;
Wherefore their bitterness to behold in me,
Malignly and unwillingly,
A bounteous and retaliating friend
Is not surprising.
The gods have methods that are various,
Not always to themselves too clear;
And mine that may destroy you or defend you

Are gentle to those of Him that you revere
So blindly while they rend you,
Till mercifully and at last they end you—
If so they do.
None of you have so long to wait
That you need be importunate,
Or too pestiferous,
In your confused assumption of a state
Not yet prepared for you.
Better prepare the state that you possess
More to the focus of your sightlessness.
So doing, you may achieve to see,
With eyes not then afraid to look at me,
How even the blind, having resumed their senses,
May seize again their few lost evidences
Of an identity.
That which I said before I say again,
As unregarded and as much in vain
As then it was:
Some would have more things done
Today than are begun—
Things that will yet, in spite of the existence
Of an unformed and misapplied assistance,

Come properly to pass;
Though hardly, I should say, by the infliction
Of insult that is organized
Inordinately for the timid fiction
Of benefits no more prized
Than in observance to be seen from here
As if they were dishonored and despised.
Bad laws are like blind pilots authorized
To see not and to care not where they steer."

All this to me was queer;
And on my tongue there was a tendency
To venture, graciously,
A syllable or an implication
That even a god might for a mortal ear,
Without immediate incineration
Of me and my interrogation,
Make his dark words more clear—
When dazzlingly, from all around,
There was a quiet lightning everywhere.
I heard what might have been the sound
Of silence burning in the air;
And there was no god there.

# SONNETS

# HAUNTED HOUSE

Here was a place where none would ever come
For shelter, save as we did from the rain.
We saw no ghost, yet once outside again
Each wondered why the other should be dumb;
For we had fronted nothing worse then gloom
And ruin, and to our vision it was plain
Where thrift, outshivering fear, had let remain
Some chairs that were like skeletons of home.

There were no trackless footsteps on the floor
Above us, and there were no sounds elsewhere.
But there was more than sound; and there was more
Than just an axe that once was in the air
Between us and the chimney, long before
Our time.   So townsmen said who found her there.

## THE SHEAVES

Where long the shadows of the wind had rolled,
Green wheat was yielding to the change assigned;
And as by some vast magic undivined
The world was turning slowly into gold.
Like nothing that was ever bought or sold
It waited there, the body and the mind;
And with a mighty meaning of a kind
That tells the more the more it is not told.

So in a land where all days are not fair,
Fair days went on till on another day
A thousand golden sheaves were lying there,
Shining and still, but not for long to stay—
As if a thousand girls with golden hair
Might rise from where they slept and go away.

# KARMA

Christmas was in the air and all was well
With him, but for a few confusing flaws
In divers of God's images.   Because
A friend of his would neither buy nor sell,
Was he to answer for the axe that fell?
He pondered; and the reason for it was,
Partly, a slowly freezing Santa Claus
Upon the corner, with his beard and bell.

Acknowledging an improvident surprise,
He magnified a fancy that he wished
The friend whom he had wrecked were here again.
Not sure of that, he found a compromise;
And from the fulness of his heart he fished
A dime for Jesus who had died for men.

## MAYA

Through an ascending emptiness of night,
Leaving the flesh and the complacent mind
Together in their sufficiency behind,
The soul of man went up to a far height;
And where those others would have had no sight
Or sense of else than terror for the blind,
Soul met the Will, and was again consigned
To the supreme illusion which is right.

"And what goes on up there," the Mind inquired,
"That I know not already to be true?"—
"More than enough, but not enough for you,"
Said the descending Soul: "Here in the dark,
Where you are least revealed when most admired,
You may still be the bellows and the spark."

# AS IT LOOKED THEN

In a sick shade of spruce, moss-webbed, rock-fed,
Where, long unfollowed by sagacious man,
A scrub that once had been a pathway ran
Blindly from nowhere and to nowhere led,
One might as well have been among the dead
As half way there alive; so I began
Like a malingering pioneer to plan
A vain return—with one last look ahead.

And it was then that like a spoken word
Where there was none to speak, insensibly
A flash of blue that might have been a bird
Grew soon to the calm wonder of the sea—
Calm as a quiet sky that looked to be
Arching a world where nothing had occurred.

## SILVER STREET

Here, if you will, your fancy may destroy
This house before you and see flaming down
To ashes and to mysteries the old town
Where Shakespeare was a lodger for Mountjoy;
Here played the mighty child who for his toy
Must have the world—king, wizard, sage and clown,
Queen, fiend and trollop—and with no more renown,
May be, than friends and envy might annoy.

And in this little grave-yard, if you will,
He stands again, as often long ago
He stood considering what it signified.
We may have doubted, or be doubting still—
But whether it be all so, or all not so,
One has to walk up Wood Street from Cheapside.

# GENEVIEVE AND ALEXANDRA

# GENEVIEVE AND ALEXANDRA

## GENEVIEVE

Why look at me so much as if today
Were the last day on earth for both of us?
Not that I'm caring on my own account—

## ALEXANDRA

Now for the love of heaven, dear Genevieve,
And for your love of me, and I'm your sister,
Say why it is that little tongue of yours,
Which God gave you to talk with and so tell
What evil it is that ails you, tells me nothing.
You sent for me as if the world were dying
All round you, quite as dogs do that are poisoned,
And here I am; and I'll be dying soon,
Of common ordinary desperation,
Unless you tell me more now in five minutes
Than I shall ferret for myself in ages.
Moreover, if you leave it all to me,
I'll make it a phenomenon so monstrous

[ 43 ]

That you may see me flying out of here
Like something scared.   What in the Lord's name is it?

GENEVIEVE

Poor child, have you no eyes?

ALEXANDRA

                    Two, Genevieve;
But they were never sharp enough to find
A way to make the man who married you
See more in me than in six hundred others.
I would have given half my fingers then
To make him look at me as if he saw me;
But it was you he saw, and you were frightened.
I wish the creature might have cared enough
To frighten me!   But I was just a thing
With skirts and arms and legs and ears and hair,
Like all the rest he saw—till he saw you.
You know it, and I say it.   That's all over.

GENEVIEVE

My God, there's no beginning to some things,
Or I could speak.   For two weeks I have waited

For you to make it easy to be hard;
And yet you tell me now that you have eyes!
Did you have eyes last night?

ALEXANDRA

I thought so.

GENEVIEVE

Yes?

ALEXANDRA

You are coming then to something, after all.
You may be coming, if one will only wait,
To what you mean.  Surely you don't mean Her?

GENEVIEVE

I'll never look to you again for words
Where I find only silence.

ALEXANDRA

Now I see:
You counted on my old unpleasant way
Of saying to you what you say to the cat.

You've always been an angel, Genevieve;
I understand, and I'll be generous.
I'm old enough, the good Lord knows, who gave me
A feature or two fewer than I could use
Of beauty, and you more than you can use;
Or so it seems.  The Lord's ways are past all
Our delving, and we've each of us a book
To read that has a leaf we'll not lay open.
It's an old game, and one Time plays with women
Who cannot meet the Lord half way.  That's you,
My angel.  There'll be something done about it;
For Time has had an eye even on you
These years together.  Don't forget old sayings,
For they are true and they have not much mercy.

### GENEVIEVE

And what's this you are saying of old sayings?
It's not the old I want now, but the new.
I've had enough that's old.  I've had enough—
Year after year of it.  Do I look old?

### ALEXANDRA

Not yet; you needn't fret.  But even at that,

There's time enough to tear the calendar
When days are dead.

GENEVIEVE

She's older than I am.

ALEXANDRA

She knows, my dear.

GENEVIEVE

She knows it, and he knows it!

ALEXANDRA

But that's not all he knows, or all she knows.

GENEVIEVE

What are you saying now?

ALEXANDRA

Dear Genevieve,
I'm saying something new.   Lord save us all,
I'm saying something new.   You cried and crumpled

[ 47 ]

For me to do it, and you only ask,
'What are you saying now?'  I'm saying this:
I'm saying there are men to take your gift
Of pride and ice and fear of being mortal,
And having it, to be happy all their days—
And others to do nothing of the sort;
I'm saying also that this man you married
Is not a cyclops or a cannibal
Who means to eat you pretty soon, even though
An alabaster shrine with now and then
A taper burning low, or going out,
Is not what he calls home, or good religion.
He calls it something else, and something worse.
I'm sorry, but he does.

GENEVIEVE

And you defend him.

ALEXANDRA

Defence and understanding, as I know them,
Are not of a necessity the same.

GENEVIEVE

How do you know so much?

ALEXANDRA

I don't know much;
I know a little.   I wish you knew a little.

GENEVIEVE

I wish you knew a little more.

ALEXANDRA

You're crying.

GENEVIEVE

Well, if I am, what of it?   I am not
The only woman who has ever cried.
I'm not the only woman, I dare say,
Who's in a cage, beating on iron bars
That even other women cannot see.

ALEXANDRA

Surely I see them—with a difference.

GENEVIEVE

How good of you to see them!

[ 49 ]

## ALEXANDRA

Genevieve,

Be quiet until you know yourself again.
You tell of cages and of iron bars,
And there are bars, I grant you: bars enough,
But they are not of iron. Do you believe,
Because a man—a rather furry man
Who likes a woman with a dash of Eve
To liven her insensible perfection—
Looks now and then the other way, that you
Are cribbed in iron for the whole blessed length
Of all your silly days? Why won't you see,
With all those eyes of yours that you don't use,
How little of what you have would be required
To send that other one to Jericho,
Or where you will? I wish I had your face!
If so, you might be free now as I am;
Free as a bird. O Lord, so free, so free!
I'll tell you what I'll do. Some day or other,
When I'm at home, I'm going to throw a brick
At that superb tall monstrous Ching-Chang vase
In the front room, which everyone admires.
There'll be a noise, and that will make a change.

You made a change, and all you get of it,
That I see, is a reason to be jealous.
Lord love us, you'll be jealous next of me,
Because your sacrificing spouse made out
Somehow to scratch my cheek with his hard whiskers
To honor my arrival.  He might as well
Have done it with a broom, and I've a guess
Would rather.

GENEVIEVE

　　　　I can only say again
I wish you knew a little more.

ALEXANDRA

　　　　　　　　　And I—
I wish you fancied less.

GENEVIEVE

　　　　　Oh, is it fancy?

ALEXANDRA

Whatever it is, you make it what it is.
I know the man.  He wants his house to live in.

[ 51 ]

He's not the sort who makes another man's
Romance a nightmare for the humor of it;
He's not one to be spinning webs of gold
As if he were a spider with an income;
He's what he is; and you that have him so,
I see, are in the best of ways to lose him.
But who am I, to talk of him?  You made me,
And you'll remember that.   Now that's all over.

GENEVIEVE

You pat me as you would a little dog.

ALEXANDRA

Of course,

GENEVIEVE

I wish you knew a little more.

ALEXANDRA

My darling, you have honored me three times
In wishing that identical sweet wish;
And if in all agreement with your text
I say as much myself and say it louder,
You'll treasure to my credit, when I'm dead,

[ 52 ]

One faint remembrance of humility.

Although I don't think you are listening,

I'm saying to you now that I'm an insect.

Lord, what a sigh!

### GENEVIEVE

I hear you—all you say;

And what you say to me so easily

May be the end of wisdom, possibly.

And I may change. I don't believe I shall,

Yet I may change—a little. I don't know.

It may be now that I don't care enough;

It may be too that I don't know enough—

To change. It may be that the few lights left

Around the shrine, as you say, may go out

Without my tending them or watching them.

It seems a jealous love is not enough

To bring at once to light, as I have seen it,

The farthest hidden of all mockeries

That home can hold and hide—until it comes.

Well, it has come. Oh, never mind me now!

Our tears are cheap, and men see few of them.

He doesn't know that I know.

## ALEXANDRA

Genevieve,
Say something, if you only say you hate me.
Poor child, I cannot ask if you are right—
Or say that you are wrong, until I find
A gleam at least of meaning in all this.
Only, remember that of all small things
That have the most infernal power to grow,
Few may be larger than a few small words
That may not say themselves and be forgotten.
No more, then.  I can live without an answer.
Indeed, I may be wrong; and it may be
That you are not my bogey-burdened sister.

## GENEVIEVE

The farthest hidden things are still, my dear.
They make no noise.  They creep from where they live
And strike us in the dark; and then we suffer.
And you my sister, of all women living,
Have made me know the truth of this I'm saying.
And you, as I'm a fool, know nothing more
Than what I've hardly said.  Thank God for that.

Why mock yourself with more unhappy names
Than sorrow shares with reason?   Why not lay
For ever, with me to help you if I can,
The last of all the bogeys you have seen
Somewhere in awful corners that are dark
Because you make them so and keep them so?
You like the dark, may be.   I don't.   I hate it.
Now tell me what it is you've 'hardly said ';
For I assure you that you've hardly said it.

## GENEVIEVE

Oh yes, I said it; and you might have heard it.
You make a jest of love, and all it means.
I can bear that.   The world has always done it,
The world has always borne it.   Many men
And women have made laughter out of those
Who might as well have been in hell as here,
Alive and listening.   When a love can hold
Its own with change no more, ' twere better then
For love to die.   There might be then, perhaps,
If that were all, an easy death for love;
If not, then for the woman.

## ALEXANDRA

                    If that were all?
You speak now as if that were not enough.


## GENEVIEVE

It seems it isn't.   There's another corner;
And in that corner there's another ghost.


## ALEXANDRA

What have I done?   Have I done anything?


## GENEVIEVE

Yes, you have made me see how poor I am;
How futile, and how far away I am
From what his hungry love and hungry mind
Thought I was giving when I gave myself.


## ALEXANDRA

But when his eyes are on you, I can swear
That I see only kindness in his eyes.


## GENEVIEVE

I'll send you home if you say that again.

## ALEXANDRA

Be tranquil; I shall not say that again.
But tell me more about his hungry mind—
I understood the rest of it.   Good Lord,
I never knew he had a hungry mind!


## GENEVIEVE

He hasn't one when you are with him.


## ALEXANDRA

What!


## GENEVIEVE

I say he hasn't one when you are with him.
You feed him.   You can talk of what he knows
And cares about.   Six years have been enough
To make what little mind I've ever had
A weariness too large for his endurance.
He knows how little I shall ever know;
He knows that in his measure I'm a fool.
And you say there's a—kindness in his eyes!
You tell me that!   I'd rather be his dog.

[ 57 ]

### ALEXANDRA

What in the name of ruin, dear Genevieve,
Do you think you are doing now with words?

### GENEVIEVE

I'd rather be a by-word in the city,
And let him have his harem and be happy.

### ALEXANDRA

It's only your too generous invention,
I'm sure, that gives him one.   I'm still about,
And I've a quick ear for iniquities.

### GENEVIEVE

To make up for an eye that's not so quick,
Most likely.   You may talk yourself to sleep
Assured that all the while I sit and listen
I shall see only kindness in his eyes.
I'd rather see him coming with a club
Than with his kindness.   Though you may not like it,
I know what I would rather do than see
Some of the things that you would have me see.

## ALEXANDRA

I'd rather you would see him as he is—
Not as a nightmare that you may have had,
Once on a time, condemns and injures him.

## GENEVIEVE

You would not have him injured for the world.
I thought so, but no matter what I thought.
I'd rather live in hovels and eat scraps,
And feed the pigs and all the wretched babies;
I'd rather steal my food from a blind man,
And give it back to him and starve to death;
I'd rather cut my feet off and eat poison;
I'd rather sit and skin myself alive
Than be a fool!  I'd rather be a toad
Than live to see that—kindness in his eyes!

## ALEXANDRA

Poor Genevieve!  Don't think that you alone
Of womankind have had these little fancies.
You are not saying this—don't imagine it.
Your nerves are talking now, and they don't know
Or care what they are saying.

**GENEVIEVE**

Never mind that.
My needs are many, but I don't need that.


**ALEXANDRA**

Poor Genevieve!


**GENEVIEVE**

And don't say that again!

# SONNETS

## A MAN IN OUR TOWN

We pitied him as one too much at ease
With Nemesis and impending indigence;
Also, as if by way of recompense,
We sought him always in extremities;
And while ways more like ours had more to please
Our common code than his improvidence,
There lurked alive in our experience
His homely genius for emergencies.

He was not one for men to marvel at,
And yet there was another neighborhood
When he was gone, and many a thrifty tear.
There was an increase in a man like that;
And though he be forgotten, it was good
For more than one of you that he was here.

## EN PASSANT

I should have glanced and passed him, naturally,
But his designs and mine were opposite;
He spoke, and having temporized a bit,
He said that he was going to the sea:
"I've watched on highways for so long," said he,
"That I'll go down there to be sure of it."
And all at once his famished eyes were lit
With a wrong light—or so it was to me.

That evening there was talk along the shore
Of one who shot a stranger, saying first:
"You should have come when called.   This afternoon
A gentleman unknown to me before,
With deference always due to souls accurst,
Came out of his own grave—and not too soon."

# NOT ALWAYS

## I

In surety and obscurity twice mailed,
And first achieving with initial rout
A riddance of weak fear and weaker doubt,
He strove alone.   But when too long assailed
By nothing, even a stronger might have quailed
As he did, and so might have gazed about
Where he could see the last light going out,
Almost as if the fire of God had failed.

And so it was till out of silence crept
Invisible avengers of a name
Unknown, like jungle-hidden jaguars.
But there were others coming who had kept
Their watch and word; and out of silence came
A song somewhat as of the morning stars.

# NOT ALWAYS

## II

There were long days when there was nothing said,
And there were longer nights where there was nought
But silence and recriminating thought
Between them like a field unharvested.
Antipathy was now their daily bread,
And pride the bitter drink they daily fought
To throw away.   Release was all they sought
Of hope, colder than moonlight on the dead.

Wishing the other might at once be sure
And strong enough to shake the prison down,
Neither believed, although they strove together,
How long the stolid fabric would endure
That was a wall for them, and was to frown
And shine for them through many sorts of weather.

# WHY HE WAS THERE

Much as he left it when he went from us
Here was the room again where he had been
So long that something of him should be seen,
Or felt—and so it was.  Incredulous,
I turned about, loath to be greeted thus,
And there he was in his old chair, serene
As ever, and as laconic and as lean
As when he lived, and as cadaverous.

Calm as he was of old when we were young,
He sat there gazing at the pallid flame
Before him.  "And how far will this go on?"
I thought.  He felt the failure of my tongue,
And smiled:  "I was not here until you came;
And I shall not be here when you are gone."

## GLASS HOUSES

Learn if you must, but do not come to me
For truth of what your pleasant neighbor says
Behind you of your looks or of your ways,
Or of your worth and virtue generally;
If he's a pleasure to you, let him be—
Being the same to him; and let your days
Be tranquil, having each the other's praise,
And each his own opinion peaceably.

Two others once did love each other well,
Yet not so well but that a pungent word
From each came stinging home to the wrong ears.
The rest would be an overflow to tell,
Surely; and you may slowly have inferred
That you may not be here a thousand years.

# MORTMAIN

# MORTMAIN

Avenel Gray at fifty had gray hair,
Gray eyes, and a gray cat—coincidence
Agreeable enough to be approved
And shared by all her neighbors; or by all
Save one, who had, in his abused esteem,
No share of it worth having.   Avenel Gray
At fifty had the favor and the grace
Of thirty—the gray hair being only a jest
Of time, he reasoned, whereby the gray eyes
Were maybe twenty or maybe a thousand.
Never could he persuade himself to say
How old or young they were, or what was in them,
Or whether in the mind or in the heart
Of their possessor there had ever been,
Or ever should be, more than room enough
For the undying dead.   All he could say
Would be that she was now to him a child,
A little frightened or a little vexed,
And now a sort of Miss Methuselah,

Adept and various in obscurity
And in omniscience rather terrible—
Until she smiled and was a child again,
Seeing with eyes that had no age in them
That his were growing older.  Seneca Sprague
At fifty had hair grayer, such as it was,
Than Avenel's—an atoll, as it were,
Circling a smooth lagoon of indignation,
Whereunder were concealed no treacheries
Or monsters that were perilous to provoke.

Seneca sat one Sunday afternoon
With Avenel in her garden.  There was peace
And languor in the air, but in his mind
There was not either—there was Avenel;
And where she was, and she was everywhere,
There was no peace for Seneca.  So today
Should see the last of him in any garden
Where a sphynx-child, with gray eyes and gray hair,
Would be the only flower that he might wish
To pluck, wishing in vain.  "I'm here again,"
Seneca said, "and I'm not here alone;
You may observe that I've a guest with me

This time, Time being the guest—scythe, glass, and all.

Time is a guest not given to long waiting,

And, in so far as you may not have known it,

I'm Destiny. For more than twenty years

My search has been for an identity

Worth Time's acknowledgment; and heretofore

My search has been but a long faltering,

Paid with an unavailing gratitude

And unconfessed encouragement from you.

What is it in me that you like so much,

And love so little? I'm not so much a monkey

As many who have had their heart's desire,

And have it still. My perishable angel,

Since neither you nor I may live forever

Like this, I'll say the folly that has fooled us

Out of our lives was never mine, but yours.

There was an understanding long ago

Between the laws and atoms that your life

And mine together were to be a triumph;

But one contingency was overlooked,

And that was a complete one. All you love,

And all you dare to love, is far from here—

Too far for me to find where I am going."

"Going? " Avenel said.  "Where are you going? "
There was a frightened wonder in her eyes
Until she found a way for them to laugh:
"At first I thought you might be going to tell me
That you had found a new way to be old—
Maybe without remembering all the time
How gray we are.  But when you soon began
To be so unfamiliar and ferocious—
Well, I began to wonder.  I'm a woman."

Seneca sighed before he shook his head
At Avenel: "You say you are a woman,
And I suppose you are.  If you are not,
I don't know what you are; and if you are,
I don't know what you mean.

                         "By what? " she said.
A faint bewildered flush covered her face,
While Seneca felt within her voice a note
As near to sharpness as a voice like hers
Might have in silent hiding.  "What have I done
So terrible all at once that I'm a stranger? "

"You are no stranger than you always were,"
He said, "and you are not required to be so.

You are no stranger now than yesterday,
Or twenty years ago; or thirty years
Longer ago than that, when you were born—
You and your brother.  I'm not here to scare you,
Or to pour any measure of reproach
Out of a surplus urn of chilly wisdom;
For watching you to find out whether or not
You shivered swallowing it would be no joy
For me.  But since it has all come to this—
Which is the same as nothing, only worse,
I am not either wise or kind enough,
It seems, to go away from you in silence.
My wonder is today that I have been
So long in finding what there was to find,
Or rather in recognizing what I found
Long since and hid with incredulities
That years have worn away, leaving white bones
Before me in a desert.  All those bones,
If strung together, would be a skeleton
That once upheld a living form of hope
For me to follow until at last it fell
Where there was only sand and emptiness.
For a long time there was not even a grave—

Hope having died there all alone, you see,
And in the dark.  And you, being as you are,
Inseparable from your obsession—well,
I went so far last evening as to fancy,
Having no other counsellor than myself
To guide me, that you might be entertained,
If not instructed, hearing how far I wandered,
Following hope into an empty desert,
And what I found there.  If we never know
What we have found, and are accordingly
Adrift upon the wreck of our invention,
We make our way as quietly to shore
As possible, and we say no more about it;
But if we know too well for our well-being
That what it is we know had best be shared
With one who knows too much of it already,
Even kindliness becomes, or may become,
A strangling and unwilling incubus.
A ghost would often help us if he could,
But being a ghost he can't.  I may confuse
Regret with wisdom, but in going so far
As not impossibly to be annoying,
My wish is that you see the part you are

Of nature.  When you find anomalies here
Among your flowers and are surprised at them,
Consider yourself and be surprised again;
For they and their potential oddities
Are all a part of nature.  So are you,
Though you be not a part that nature favors,
And favoring, carries on.  You are a monster;
A most adorable and essential monster."


He watched her face and waited, but she gave him
Only a baffled glance before there fell
So great a silence there among the flowers
That even their fragrance had almost a sound;
And some that had no fragrance may have had,
He fancied, an accusing voice of color
Which her pale cheeks now answered with another;
Wherefore he gazed a while at tiger-lilies
Hollyhocks, dahlias, asters and hydrangeas—
The generals of an old anonymous host
That he knew only by their shapes and faces.
Beyond them he saw trees; and beyond them
A still blue summer sky where there were stars
In hiding, as there might somewhere be veiled

Eternal reasons why the tricks of time
Were played like this.  Two insects on a leaf
Would fill about as much of nature's eye,
No doubt, as would a woman and a man
At odds with heritage.  Yet there they sat,
A woman and a man, beyond the range
Of all deceit and all philosophy
To make them less or larger than they were.
The sun might only be a spark among
Superior stars, but one could not help that.

"If a grim God that watches each of us
In turn, like an old-fashioned schoolmaster,"
Seneca said, still gazing at the blue
Beyond the trees, "no longer satisfies,
Or tortures our credulity with harps
Or fires, who knows if there may not be laws
Harder for us to vanquish or evade
Than any tyrants?  Rather, we know there are;
Or you would not be studying butterflies
While I'm encouraging Empedocles
In retrospect.  He was a mountain-climber,
You may remember; and while I think of him,

I think if only there were more volcanoes,
More of us might be climbing to their craters
To find out what he found.  You are sufficient,
You and your cumulative silences
Today, to make of his abysmal ashes
The dust of all our logic and our faith;
And since you can do that, you must have power
That you have never measured.  Or, if you like,
A power too large for any measurement
Has done it for you, made you as you are,
And led me for the last time, possibly,
To bow before a phantom in your garden."
He smiled—until he saw tears in her eyes,
And then remarked, "Here comes a friend of yours.
Pyrrhus, you call him.  Pyrrhus because he purrs."

"I found him reading Hamlet," Avenel said;
"By which I mean that I was reading Hamlet.
But he's an old cat now.  And I'm another—
If you mean what you say, or seem to say.
If not, what in the world's name do you mean?"

He met the futile question with a question
Almost as futile and almost as old:

"Why have I been so long learning to read,
Or learning to be willing to believe
That I was learning?  All that I had to do
Was to remember that your brother once
Was here, and is here still.  Why have I waited—
Why have you made me wait—so long to say so? "
Although he said it kindly, and foresaw
That in his kindness would be pain, he said it—
More to the blue beyond the trees, perhaps,
Or to the stars that moved invisibly
To laws implacable and inviolable,
Than to the stricken ears of Avenel,
Who looked at him as if to speak.  He waited,
Until it seemed that all the leaves and flowers,
The butterflies and the cat, were waiting also.

"Am I the only woman alive," she asked,
"Who has a brother she may not forget?
If you are here to be mysterious,
Ingenuousness like mine may disappoint you.
And there are women somewhere, certainly,
Riper for mysteries than I am yet.
You see me living always in one place,

And all alone."

        "No, you are not alone,"

Seneca said: "I wish to God you were!

And I wish more that you had been so always,

That you might be so now. Your brother is here,

And yet he has not been here for ten years.

Though you've a skill to crowd your paradigms

Into a cage like that, and keep them there,

You may not yet be asking quite so much

Of others, for whom the present is not the past.

We are not all magicians; and Time himself

Who is already beckoning me away,

Would surely have been cut with his own scythe,

And long ago, if he had followed you

In all your caprioles and divagations.

You have deceived the present so demurely

That only few have been aware of it,

And you the least of all. You do not know

How much it was of you that was not you

That made me wait. And why I was so long

In seeing that it was never to be you,

Is not for you to tell me—for I know.

I was so long in seeing it was not you,

[ 81 ]

Because I would not see.  I wonder, now,
If I should take you up and carry you off,
Like an addressable orang-outang,
You might forget the grave where half of you
Is buried alive, and where the rest of you,
Whatever you may believe it may be doing,
Is parlously employed."   As if to save
His mistress the convention of an answer,
The cat jumped up into her lap and purred,
Folded his paws, and looked at Seneca
Suspiciously.  "I might almost have done it,"
He said, "if insight and experience
Had not assured me it would do no good.
Don't be afraid.  I have tried everything,
Only to be assured it was not you
That made me fail.  If you were here alone,
You would not see the last of me so soon;
And even with you and the invisible
Together, maybe I might have seized you then
Just hard enough to leave you black and blue—
Not that you would have cared one way or other,
With him forever near you, and if unseen,
Always a refuge.  No, I should not have hurt you.

It would have done no good—yet might perhaps
Have made me likelier to be going away
At the right time.   Anyhow, damn the cat."

Seneca looked at Avenel till she smiled,
And so let loose a tear that she had held
In each of her gray eyes.   "I am too old,"
She said, "and too incorrigibly alone,
For you to laugh at me.   You have been saying
More nonsense in an hour than I have heard
Before in forty years.   Why do you do it?
Why do you talk like this of going away?
Where would you be, and what would you be doing?
You would be like a cat in a strange house—
Like Pyrrhus here in yours.   I have not had
My years for nothing; and you are not so young
As to be quite so sure that I'm a child.
We are too old to be ridiculous,
And we've been friends too long."

                                "We have been friends
Too long," he said, "to be friends any longer.
And there you have the burden of a song
That I came here to sing this afternoon.

When I said friends you might have halted me,
For I meant neighbors."

                        "I know what you meant,"
Avenel answered, gazing at the sky,
And then at Seneca. "The great question is,
What made you say it? You mention powers and laws,
As if you understood them. Am I stranger
Than powers and laws that make me as I am? "


"God knows you are no stranger than you are,
For which I praise Him," Seneca said, devoutly.
"I see no need of prayer to bring to pass
For me more prodigies or more difficulties.
I cry for them no longer when I know
That you are married to your brother's ghost,
Even as you were married to your brother—
Never contending or suspecting it,
Yet married all the same. You are alone,
But only in so far as to my eyes
The sight of your beloved is unseen.
Why should I come between you and your ghost,
Whose hand is always chilly on my shoulder,
Drawing me back whenever I go forward?

I should have been acclaimed stronger than he
Before he died, but he can twist me now,
And I resign my dream to his dominion.
And if by chance of an uncertain urge
Of weariness or pity you might essay
The stranglings of a twofold loyalty,
The depth and length and width of my estate,
Measured magnanimously, would be but that
Of half a grave. I'd best be rational,
I'm saying therefore to myself today,
And leave you quiet. I can originate
No reason larger than a leucocyte
Why you should not, since there are two of you,
Be tranquil here together till the end."

"You would not tell me this if it were true,
And I, if it were true, should not believe it,"
Said Avenel, stroking slowly with cold hands
The cat's warm coat. "But I might still be vexed—
Yes, even with you; and that would be a pity.
It may be well for you to go away—
Or for a while—perhaps. I have not heard
Such an unpleasant nonsense anywhere

As this of yours.  I like you, Seneca,
But not when you bring Time and Destiny,
As now you do, for company.  When you come
Some other day, leave your two friends outside.
We have gone well without them for so long
That we shall hardly be tragedians now,
Not even if we may try; and we have been
Too long familiar with our differences
To quarrel—or to change."

               Avenel smiled
At Seneca with gray eyes wherein were drowned
Inquisitive injuries, and the gray cat yawned
At him as he departed with a sigh
That answered nothing.  He went slowly home,
Imagining, as a fond improvisation,
That waves huger than Andes or Sierras
Would soon be overwhelming, as before,
A ship that would be sunk for the last time
With all on board, and far from Tilbury Town.

# SONNETS

## THE LAGGARDS

Scorners of earth, you that have one foot shod
With skyward wings, but are not flying yet,
You that observe no goal or station set
Between your groping and the towers of God
For which you languish, may it not be odd
And avaricious of you to forget
Your toll of an accumulating debt
For dusty leagues that you are still to plod?

But many have paid, you say, and paid again;
And having had worse than death are still alive,
Only to pay seven fold, and seven times seven.
They are many; and for cause not always plain,
They are the laggards among those who strive
On earth to raise the golden dust of heaven.

# NEW ENGLAND

Here where the wind is always north-north-east
And children learn to walk on frozen toes,
Wonder begets an envy of all those
Who boil elsewhere with such a lyric yeast
Of love that you will hear them at a feast
Where demons would appeal for some repose,
Still clamoring where the chalice overflows
And crying wildest who have drunk the least.

Passion is here a soilure of the wits,
We're told, and Love a cross for them to bear;
Joy shivers in the corner where she knits
And Conscience always has the rocking-chair,
Cheerful as when she tortured into fits
The first cat that was ever killed by Care.

## "IF THE LORD WOULD MAKE WINDOWS
IN HEAVEN"

She who had eyes but had not wherewithal
To see that he was doomed to his own way,
Dishonored his illusions day by day,
And year by year was more angelical.
Flaunting an injured instinct for the small,
She stifled always more than she would say;
Nursing a fear too futile to betray,
She sewed, and waited for the roof to fall.

A seer at home, she saw that his high lights
That were not shining, and were not afire,
Were such as never would be seen from there;
A saint abroad, she saw him on the heights,
And feared for him—who, if he went much higher,
Might one day not be seen from anywhere.

## BATTLE AFTER WAR

Out of a darkness, into a slow light
That was at first no light that had a name,
Like one thrust up from Erebus he came,
Groping alone, blind with remembered sight.
But there were not those faces in the night,
And all those eyes no longer were aflame
That once he feared and hated, being the same
As his that were the fuel of his fright.

He shone, for one so long among the lost,
Like a stout Roman after Pentecost:
"Terror will yield as much as we dare face
Ourselves in it, and it will yield no more,"
He said.  And we see two now in his place,
Where there was room for only one before.

# THE GARDEN OF THE NATIONS

## (1923)

When we that are the bitten flower and fruit
Of time's achievement are undone between
The blight above, where blight has always been,
And the old worm of evil at the root,
We shall not have to crumble destitute
Of recompense, or measure our chagrin;
We shall be dead, and so shall not be seen
Amid the salvage of our disrepute.

And when we are all gone, shall mightier seeds
And scions of a warmer spring put forth
A bloom and fruitage of a larger worth
Than ours?  God save the garden, if by chance,
Or by approved short sight, more numerous weeds
And weevils be the next inheritance!

# REUNION

By some derision of wild circumstance
Not then our pleasure somehow to perceive,
Last night we fell together to achieve
A light eclipse of years.   But the pale chance
Of youth resumed was lost.   Time gave a glance
At each of us, and there was no reprieve;
And when there was at last a way to leave,
Farewell was a foreseen extravagance.

Tonight the west has yet a failing red,
While silence whispers of all things not here;
And round there where the fire was that is dead,
Dusk-hidden tenants that are chairs appear.
The same old stars will soon be overhead,
But not so friendly and not quite so near.

# DEMOS AND DIONYSUS

# DEMOS AND DIONYSUS

### DIONYSUS

Good morning, Demos.

### DEMOS

    I thought you were dead.

### DIONYSUS

If you look too assuredly for death
To consummate your preference and desire,
Sometime you may endure, to your surprise
The pang of an especial disappointment.
Why such a fever of unfriendliness?
And why, again, so brief a courtesy?

### DEMOS

There was no courtesy. Had I the power
To crown my will with its accomplishment,
The crowning would be brief enough, God knows.

### DIONYSUS

And you would then be king.

### DEMOS

                              Say as you like,
Your words are of a measure with your works.

### DIONYSUS

If you assume with me too large a license,
How do you know that you may not be seized
With one of my more celebrated frenzies
And eat yourself alive?  If you do that,
Who then shall be the king that shall inherit
The realm that is your envy and the dream
Of your immoderate magnificence?

### DEMOS

There are to be no kings where I shall reign.

### DIONYSUS

Not so?   Then how are you to do your reigning?
I'm asking only as an eager child

Might ask as much of an impatient father.
We'll say a patient and unusual child,
Not listening always for a sudden answer.

### DEMOS

Your days are as the pages of a book,
And one where Finis waits for no long reading.

### DIONYSUS

You are somewhat irrelevant, and too hasty,
But that's to be forgiven of a king.
The king can do no wrong.  As for the book
Where Finis waits, how far along are you
In reading it, and thereby in absorbing
The indemnifying gist of what it means?

### DEMOS

I have read far enough to find in it
No sure indemnity save one of grief,
And one of death.

### DIONYSUS

Nothing of life at all?

### Demos

Nothing of life to me.

### Dionysus

How came you then
So neutrally and unecstatically
At one time to be born?

### Demos

I do not see
More than some words in that.

### Dionysus

I know you don't,
The book of what you do not see, my friend,
Would have no Finis in it.   Your dim faith—
Your faith in something somewhere out of nothing—
And your industrious malevolence
Against yourself and the divine escape
That makes a wine of water when it will—
Or not, if it will not—may soon or late
Consume your folly to a long fatigue,

And to an angry death.   You measure me
By something in a flagon or a glass—
And we're away from that.   Leaving aside
The lesser and the larger mysteries,
By what obscured immeasurable means
Are you to have in your attractive prison
The music of the world and of the stars
Without me, or to make of love and art
The better part—without me?   Do you know?

### DEMOS

I do not see the prison.

### DIONYSUS

But you will;
And having filled it you may blow it up
In the necessity of desperation.

### DEMOS

I do not know your language; and far less
Do I concede with you in love and art
The better part.

#### Dionysus

And that you never will.

#### Demos

I hope not.

#### Dionysus

All you hope will come to pass,
If you achieve your way.  You stamp your coin
Of words too small to compass their design,
Or to authenticate their currency.

#### Demos

Yet somehow they are current.

#### Dionysus

So they are;
And so are the uncounted flying seeds
Of death for you to breathe and eat and drink,
Never aware of their ascendency
Till you are down where they're devouring you
And you are groaning to be rid of them.

DEMOS

There are physicians.

DIONYSUS

There are not so many
That you may trust them for immunity
From your disease, or pay them for a cure
With your ingenious coin.   Under your sway
They would all be as easily indisposed
As you are now, and at as blind a loss
To say what ailed them.   Given release enough,
They might arrive, in a combined rebellion,
At some unethical unanimity
As to the poison most expedient
For the accomplishment of your transition,
But they would never cure you otherwise;
And they will never make you less the monster
That you would be, and may be—for a time.
There are futilities and enormities
That must be loved and honored and obeyed
Before they are found out.   If you be one,
Or other, or both, as I believe you are,

[ 103 ]

God help the credulous and expectant slaves
Of your unconscionable supremacy.


DEMOS

They are expectant, certainly, and wisely;
My argument enfolds them and assures them.


DIONYSUS

And obfuscates their proper sight of you.
In your forensic you are not unlike
The pleasant and efficient octopus,
Who inks the sea around him with a cloud
That hides his most essential devilishness,
Leaving his undulating tentacles
To writhe and shoot and strangle as they may.


DEMOS

By turning your two eyes to land again
You may regard some hundred million souls
Or more that are awaiting my tuition—
Where Reason and Equality, like strong twins,
Will soon be brother giants, overseeing

[ 104 ]

Incessantly the welfare of them all.
A little strangling will be good for them,
And they will have no courage to complain.

DIONYSUS

They will not have their souls by then.  By then,
You and your twins—both illegitimate,
And the most credible liars ever conceived—
Will have reduced their souls to common fuel,
And their obedient selves to poor machines
That ultimately will disintegrate,
Leaving you outcast and discredited,
A king of ruins; though you are not yet worse
Than a malignant and a specious warning—
Albeit you may attain to your desire
If it be fate that you shall be the scourge
Of a slave-ridden state for long enough
To prove and alienate your demonship
Till you are done with.  In the mixed meantime,
A thousand men, had they the will to speak,
Might shred your folly to its least of words
And thereby have the ruin less methodized
If not forestalled and thwarted.  You may smile

[ 105 ]

Till you may be as far from recognition
As from a reason why a man should live,
But you will be no lovelier than for that
Than you are now.   Why do you wet your lips
With your mendacious tongue, and rub your hands?

## DEMOS

Why do I smile?   Why do I rub my hands?
Because your thousand men will never speak.
I have you there, my master.   Some will curse
Among themselves a little; some will grunt;
Others will shrug their unoffending shoulders
At my offensive name; others will stretch
Themselves, and in the refuge of a yawn
Will say they have enough to last their time
And that the future must attend itself—
As you foresee it will.   They are all safe,
And comfortably gagged.   They will not speak—
Or not more than a few—and fewer still
Will act; and those who do may do no more
Than a few shipwrecked generals on an island
Might do if they were all to draw their swords
At once, and then make faces and throw stones

At my perfidious and indifferent image.
I fear, my master, you are left behind.
One of these days, the world will be a hive—
The veritable asylum you deplore
So vainly now.   Then every little bee
Will have his little task, and having done it,
His time to play.   So all will be in order,
And the souring hopes of individuals
To be some day themselves, though God knows how,
Will all be sweetened with synthetic honey.
The waste of excellence that you call art
Will be a thing remembered as a toy
Dug somewhere from forgotten history;
And this infirmity that you name love
Will be subdued to studious procreation.

DIONYSUS

Of what?

DEMOS

Why, of Reason and Equality.

DIONYSUS

Your twins again.   With you for the king-bee,
And with an army of converted drones

[ 107 ]

Stinging your hive to order, as you say,
Where then would be the purpose or the need
Of any such hive?   Were it not better now,
Beforehand, to forestall monotony
And servitude with one complete carouse,
Capped with a competent oblivion—
Or with a prayer at least for such an end?
If in the sorry picture that you flaunt
Before me as your ultimate panorama
Of an invertebrate futility
You see no reason to be sick at heart,—
I do.   I see a reason to shed tears.
What will be left in your millennium
When self and soul are gone and all subdued
Insensibly?

### DEMOS

Self and soul will not be missed,
Having been rather too much in the way,
And too long, for the good of the machine,
In which I see an end and a beginning.
Men have been playing heretofore too much
With feeling and with unprofitable fancy.

### DIONYSUS

I see an end, but not yet the beginning.
Feeling and fancy?   What do you know of them?

### DEMOS

Enough to say that in the kingdom coming—
O yes, I shall be king—they shall be whipped
And rationed into reason.   Where a few
That are peculiar would precede the many,
Measures are always waiting.

### DIONYSUS

                                If there be not
A few that are peculiar in your world,
Your world will be a more peculiar place
Than all your nightmares have inhabited;
And howsoever you compel your zeal
To swallow your deceit, I'll apprehend
Their presence even in your machinery.
Something will break if they are not subdued,

### DEMOS

They will be ground to death if they are there,
And in the way.

### DIONYSUS

And if the machine breaks
In breaking them, who patches the machine?
You and your amiable automatons
Will have no more the feeling or the fancy
To prove or guess what ails it.

### DEMOS

The machine,
Once running, will run always.  As for you,
You will be driven off somewhere from the world,
And in some hell of exile and remembrance
Will see how it all goes, and how securely
The mechanistic hive subdues itself
To system and to order—and to Reason.

### DIONYSUS

And to Equality.  How do you know today
That I may not return again from hell—
Acceptably, perchance—and bring some honey?

### DEMOS

Your sort of honey will have no taste then
For palates that are duly neutralized;

[ 110 ]

And all its evil sweet and stickiness
Will be a freight for you to ferry back
To the same place where you discovered it.


DIONYSUS

Why do you so invidiously insist
That I shall go so far—or that my honey
Is half so evil or so inimical
As that of your abject anticipation?


DEMOS

Abject?   I do not wholly see it so.


DIONYSUS

It must have been the milder side of me
That held a lodging for so mild a word.
While I consider the complaint slaves
That you would have subdued to your machine,
I beg your mechanistic leave to shudder,
For your "subdued" pursues me.

[ 111 ]

### DEMOS

As in due time
It will for certain seize you and arraign you
For what you are.

### DIONYSUS

Would that it might do so!
Yet that's the one of all things onerous
And easy that will not be done for me.
Simplicity was not my father's name,
Nor was it ever mine; yet I'm unfeigned
To see, for those who may.   My mother died
Because she would see God.   I did not die.
Was it not strange that I should be twice born
For nothing, if I be what you make of me—
A lord of life that has no worthier fate
Than one of hell, with death and evil honey
For my companionship and consolation?

### DEMOS

I have not made of you a lord of life;
And as for recommending hell and honey,

[ 112 ]

There may be one for you without the other.
We shall have neither here.

### DIONYSUS

                    I'm of a mind
To prophecy that you may have the one
And hunger for the other, till presently
You shall have both again, as you do now.
My way would not be yours; and my machine
Would have a more forbearing alternation
Attending a less dread beneficence.

### DEMOS

What do you mean by that?

### DIONYSUS

                    I mean as much
As an observing child might understand
Who grows to see between him and another
A living difference and an impetus
To breathe and be himself.   I mean, also,
An increment of reason not like yours,
Which is the crucifixion of all reason,

But one that quickens in the seed of truth
And is the flower of truth—not always fair,
Yet always to be found if you will see it.
There *is* a Demos, and you know his name
By force of easy stealing; yet his face
Would be one of a melancholy stranger
To you if he saw yours.  I know his face,
And why he keeps it hidden until the wreck
Of your invention shall betray itself
As a monstrosity beyond repair,
And only by slow toil to be removed.
I mean that all your frantic insolence
Of hate and of denatured eagerness
To build in air a solid monument
From the wrong end will end in a collapse,
With you beneath it bellowing for relief
Not interested or available.
I mean that of all noxious tyrannies
Potential in imaginable folly,
The tyrant of the most intolerable
And unenduring will obscure himself
With much the same suave and benevolent mask
As this that you are wearing now to cover

The guile you dare not show to your disciples.
I mean that your delirious clumsy leap
From reason to the folly you call reason
Will only make of you and of your dupes
A dislocated and unlovely mess
For undertakers, who are not yet born
To view the coming ruin that is to be
Their occupation and emolument—
If your delusion for a time prevail,
As like enough it will. I mean, also,
That after suffering time has had enough
Of you and of your sterile dispensation,
Some wholesome fire of thought and competence
Will make of what is left a cannistered
Memorial of unlovely orts and ashes,
To be a warning and a wonderment
Where you shall plot no more. I mean a world
Fit for a self-defending human race
To recognize, and finally to live in.

DEMOS

I'll put the clamps on harder, just for that,
And let you see what Reason really is,

In fact and action.  We have had too much
Of the insurgent individual
With his free fancy and free this and that,
And his ingenuous right to be himself.
What right has anyone now to be himself
Since I am here to fix him in his place
And hold him there?   And as for your fit world,
I'll have it all alike and of a piece—
Punctual, accurate, tamed and uniform,
And equal.   Then romance and love and art
And ecstasy will be remembrances
Of man's young weakness on his way to reason.
When my world's once in order, you shall see.

DIONYSUS

I may, but God forbid the sight of it.
I'd rather stay in hell, which you imply
To be preparing for me.

DEMOS

                    I approve
Unspeakably of such a preference
On your part.   Go at once, for all I care,
And stay.

### DIONYSUS

I may go somewhere, for a while,
But I am one of those who have perforce
To live and to return.   Should there be need
Of me, I may remain; and you may find
One day a merry welcome waiting you
In the same place where you say I belong:
Take off your mask and find another name,
Or I'll be sure you will.   Good morning, Demos.

### DEMOS

Good morning, Dionysus.   Wait and see.

F